KEEPING THE PEACE

Keeping the Peace

MINDFULNESS AND PUBLIC SERVICE

Thich Nhat Hanh

PARALLAX PRESS

BERKELEY, CALIFORNIA

Parallax Press
P.O. Box 7355
Berkeley, California 94707
www.parallax.org

Parallax Press is the publishing division
of Unified Buddhist Church, Inc.

This book is taken from talks given at the "Protecting
and Serving Without Stress or Fear" retreat at Green
Lake, Wisconsin in August of 2003.
Edited by Rachel Neumann.
Cover and text design by Gopa & Ted 2, Inc.
Back cover photo by Nang Sao.

Library of Congress Cataloging-in-Publication Data

Nhât Hanh, Thích.
  Keeping the peace : mindfulness & public service /
Thich Nhat Hanh.
     p. cm.
  ISBN 1-888375-48-5 (pbk.)
  1. Peace of mind—Religious aspects—Buddhism.
  2. Spiritual life—Buddhism. 3. Quality of work
life—United States. 4. Police-community relations—
United States. 5. Buddhism—Social aspects.
I. Title.
  BQ4570.P4N454 2005
  294.3'37631—dc22

2005004055

3 4 5 6 7 / 13 12 11 10 09

Table of Contents

SECTION 3: PEACE IN THE WORLD

Foreword

WHEN I BECAME a police officer in 1984, my deepest aspiration was to work for peace and to end violence and injustice. I quickly became intimately familiar, on a nightly basis, with the suffering caused by poverty, racism, social injustice, stealing, sexual abuse, domestic abuse, unmindful consumption, and oppression. I deeply craved peace, but I did not understand that peace began in my own heart. I felt overwhelmed by the suffering I witnessed, by public misunderstanding, and by the politics of my own department. The misplaced anger of others fanned my own impatience and anger. I began to do my job in a mechanical way. I consumed too much alcohol, and I became angry and depressed. As a result, I brought suffering into my relationships with my family and others.

I was curious but skeptical when I attended my first retreat with Thich Nhat Hanh in 1991. At that retreat, he and Sister Chan Kong convinced me that it was possible to carry a gun mindfully. I left the retreat believing I could integrate my public service and mindfulness. Slowly, over the next fourteen years, with the support of my local and international community, I began to develop my practice of mindfulness. With time, I was able to let go of my cynicism and open my heart.

I am still unskillful at times, but this experience of opening up to my sad and tender heart produced a fearlessness that enabled me to begin the process of transforming myself. I found the compassion that comes with being willing to be vulnerable and touched by the world. I also learned that being effective did not depend on my authority but, instead, depended on a larger coordinated effort to bring about peace in myself, my family, my workplace, and my community.

A non-sectarian retreat, held in August of 2003 at Green Lake, Wisconsin, called "Protecting and Serving Without Stress or Fear," serves as the foundation of this book. It was a deeply transformative retreat, as public safety professionals shared deeply with others the fears and suffering they deal with every day as part of their jobs.

This remarkable retreat also demonstrated the healing and peace-making power of community. Not long after attending the retreat, a woman was walking down a street in Madison, Wisconsin and witnessed two police officers arresting somebody and putting him into the back of a squad car. After closing the squad car's door, the officers turned, recognized the person from the retreat, and calmly and mindfully bowed, creating an island of peace and support in what otherwise could have been a chaotic moment.

Also noteworthy is the immeasurable gratitude I have for my spiritual community, the Snowflower Sangha. Without the dedicated hard work and deep support of so many Sangha members, this transformative retreat simply could not have occurred. If the retreat had not occurred, many seeds of peace would not have been watered. And this book might not be in your hands. It was a rich lesson in the power of community to create peace.

This book is not just for those in public service. Rather, it teaches all of us how to use mindfulness to maintain a balance of action, contemplation, and interaction in our lives. It will inspire you to create a sense of community and shared vision in your workplace. I firmly believe that our successful efforts will decrease the need for police involvement, prisons, wars, and even terrorist activities.

I bow to each person who reads this book and to the potential it will create in all of us to bring peace to ourselves, our communities, and the world. I offer a lotus to you, a buddha to be.

—Cheri Maples, Administrator of Community Corrections
for the State of Wisconsin

Introduction

Becoming Officers of Peace

THIS BOOK is dedicated to those whose job it is to keep the peace. You may think that this does not include you. But police officers, corrections officers, and judges are not the only ones who practice law enforcement. As teachers, parents, and members of our community, we all must work to create and sustain peace.

This book uses the ideas of the Buddha and the Dharma to bring peace and mindfulness to people at work. What is Dharma? Dharma is the kind of insight, practice, and code of behavior that will bring about mutual understanding, compassion, peace, and happiness. Dharma is a Sanskrit term that can be translated as "law." The practice of the Dharma is also the practice of law enforcement.

To understand what is happening to us at work, we need to look at our home life and our families. A family is a living organism that has the capacity to protect and heal itself. All living organisms have the capacity for mindfulness. When a virus penetrates the body of an organism, the body is mindful that it has been invaded. Antibodies are ready to resist the invader. The immune system is an agent of protection. If there are not enough antibodies, the immune system quickly produces more in order to cope with the invasion and sustain itself. In this way, the immune system is a reflection of the body's mindfulness.

The practice of mindfulness helps us to build an immune system for our family. Suppose your child is suffering. If you are too preoccupied with other things, and your child is not able to handle the problem alone, he or she will try to ignore and disguise the suffering inside with unhealthy behavior. Unresolved suffering can affect the entire family. If we can embrace our family's suffering, as well as our own, then we can begin to heal.

There is a way to transform suffering and free ourselves from it. In order to find the way out, we must first understand the nature and origin of our own suffering. Once we have begun this work within ourselves, we can bring our understanding into our work environment, and use it to help the larger community whom we serve in our work. The needs of our personal life are not separate from those of our work life. Our inability to be mindful and bring our full attention to what we are doing has both personal and professional costs.

Beginning this healing at home will help us understand our situations at work, particularly if we work in public service or other high-stress occupations. If we are mindful, we can be fully present at work. Our work can become our community, giving us a foundation of strength and support as we begin doing service in the larger world.

As a person working in public service, you may be inspired to act like a Buddha, someone who is filled with compassion and calm. This book offers insights and concrete practices for transformation and healing. It is set up in a simple way, to make it easy to follow the path of mindfulness and compassion. The first section focuses on your own transformation and healing, cultivating compassion and understanding for yourself. You cannot understand or help others until you help yourself. The second section focuses on becoming a bodhisattva, a Buddha bringing the practice into your work environment and sharing it in your community. When you have succeeded in building a beautiful community you are in a position to help the people that you serve. The third section focuses on the ways in which we can make not only ourselves more peaceful, but make the world we live in more peaceful as well. We can all become officers of peace, no matter what our profession.

SECTION 1

❧ *Peace in Ourselves*

1 Being in the Here and Now

Workplace Practice: Walking Meditation

"ALTHOUGH I DON'T PROFESS TO BE NORMAL,
I AM HUMAN AS ARE ALL THE OTHER PEOPLE I WORK WITH,
AND SOMETIMES EVEN I FORGET THAT."
—*Violent Crimes Investigator, Flagstaff, Arizona*

ONE DAY a journalist from French television came to report on the life and practice in Plum Village, the practice center where I live in France. When he came there were many people in Plum Village: monks, nuns, and also laypeople with families and children. Before he interviewed the monks, nuns, and laypeople, we invited him to join our practice of mindful walking. Mindful walking is a practice we do every day. We just walk, one foot in front of the other, paying attention to each breath. It is a simple practice, but it brings us much joy.

There were hundreds of people walking with us that morning, including many children. The walk lasted about forty-five minutes. I held the hands of two children as I walked. They helped me feel refreshed, and I passed on to them my solidity and peace. I enjoyed the walk very much, but the television journalist did not enjoy it at all. Later on, he described the walk as being "exhausting." In fact, we had not made any strenuous effort. We had just enjoyed making steps, touching the Earth and the wonders of life that are present in the here and now. It seemed that the journalist was used to running and was not able to stop and to be in the here and now. There was a strong energy in him, pushing him ahead, causing him to think of this and that. The morning had been very beautiful: birds were singing and many children were out playing. Perhaps he was thinking about writing and worried about completing the report for his television network. He was not free to enjoy the beautiful morning.

Cultivating Happiness

The basic condition of happiness is freedom. If there is something on your mind that you keep thinking about, then you are caught and have no freedom. If you are caught in sorrow and regret about the past, or if you are anxious about what will happen to you in the future, then you are not really free to enjoy the many wonders of life that are available in the here and now. The blue sky, the beautiful trees, the lovely faces of children, the flowers, and the birds can nourish and heal us in the present moment.

Many people in our society are not happy, even though the conditions for their happiness already exist. Their "habit energy" is always pushing them ahead, preventing them from being happy in the here and now. But with a little bit of training, we can all learn to recognize this energy every time it comes up. Why wait to be happy?

If our journalist had received some instructions and training in mindful walking, he would have been able to enjoy the walk with us. But because his mind was preoccupied with finishing the report so he could go home, he was impatient. When you walk, it is possible to walk in such a way that every step becomes nourishing and healing. This is not difficult. Whether you are a businessperson walking across the office, a congressperson walking up the Capitol steps, or a police officer out on the streets, it is always possible to practice mindful walking and to enjoy every step you take. If you know the art of mindful walking, then you will be fully present in the here and now. You make yourself available to life and life becomes available to you.

Every one of us has the tendency to run. We have run all of our lives, and we continue to run into the future where we think that some happiness may be waiting. We have received the habit of running from our parents and ancestors. When we learn to recognize our habit of running, we can use mindful breathing, and simply smile at this habit and say: "Hello, my dear old friend, I know you are there." And then you are free from this habit energy. You don't have to fight it. There is no fighting in this practice. There is only recognition and awareness of what is going on. When the habit energy of running manifests itself, you just smile and come back to your mindful breathing. Then you are free from it, and you continue to breathe in, breathe out, and enjoy the present moment.

LIVING IN MINDFULNESS

Mindfulness is the kind of energy that helps you to be fully present, to live life in the here and now. Every one of us can generate the energy of mindfulness. When you breathe in and out, if you focus on the air passing through your body, this is called mindful breathing. When you drink a glass of water, focusing all your attention on drinking and not thinking of anything else, this is called mindful drinking. When you walk and pay attention only to the steps you make and nothing else, this is called mindful walking.

Perhaps you think this is nice, but that it can only happen if you are on vacation or outside in the country. In fact, it can happen anywhere. If you are a police officer and have to spend a lot of time on the street, you might like to enjoy the practice of mindful walking. Why not? You have to pay attention and do your job, but you can also notice the good people, trees, and birds out on the street. You can enjoy meeting people. And you can look at them as friends, as the object of your work, because your duty is to protect them, and be their friend. Smile to the people you meet in the street, because you know that they need you. And it is possible for the rest of us to look at a police officer as a friend because we know that we need law enforcement. So don't think only of the danger you might find on the street. You can also think about the positive things. Teachers, librarians, social workers—all of you spend some time at work walking around, even if it is just watching children at lunchtime or visiting a client in their home. Walking meditation is a wonderful way to get in touch with the positive elements of life that are available within and around us.

If you are a health professional—a doctor, a nurse, a therapist, a social worker, or an emergency medical technician—you have to be in touch with many people who are ill and suffering. The practice of walking meditation can give you strength by helping you see the wonders of life. Walking in the street, don't think only about accidents that may happen. You have to focus your attention on the positive things, also, and then when there is difficulty, you will be ready to confront it.

Suppose you need to be at the airport at ten o'clock. You think that you have time to linger and wait until later to leave your house. But maybe there is heavy traffic, and you arrive late, and you have to run. You can always plan so that you have plenty of time to walk as a free person at the airport. Give yourself an extra hour in order to have the pleasure of doing walking meditation at the airport. Wherever we are, we can always go from one building to another with the pleasure of walking meditation. So, it should become a habit to plan in such a way that we have plenty of time to do each thing. That's a good habit that everyone can have.

Mindful walking is my practice. Every time I walk, I walk with mindfulness. Everyone can do that. In my community in France, the whole community practices mindful walking. Whether they go to the kitchen, meditation hall, or restroom, they always apply the techniques and art of mindful walking, learning how to live deeply in every moment of daily life.

✑§ *Workplace Practice: Walking Meditation*

There are two kinds of walking meditation. The first is slow walking. If your job has you sitting inside all day, you can try this by going for a walk on your lunch break, even if the walk is just around the block! You may like to practice slow walking at home in your back yard. Slow walking is especially helpful for beginners. As you breathe in, take one step. When you breathe out, take another step. Bring full attention to the contact between your foot and the ground. Breathing in, you make one step with your left foot. You can say to yourself: "I have arrived." This is not a declaration, this is a practice. You have to really arrive. "Arrive where?" you may ask. Arrive in the here and now. According to this teaching and practice, life is available only in the here and now. The past is already gone. The future is not yet here. There is only one moment when you can be truly alive, and that is the present moment.

Your step brings you back to the present so that you can touch the wonders of life in that moment. You have made an appointment with life for the here and now. If you miss the present moment, you miss your appointment with life. Mindful walking is a wonderful way to learn and train ourselves to live in the here and now. It means being truly alive. If you are carried away by the past, if you are carried away by the future, you are not really living your life. Only by deeply touching the present moment can you touch true life and be truly alive.

Don't think that you have to "be a Buddhist" or understand everything about mindfulness right away. All you need is willingness, and you will be able to arrive in the here and now. When you breathe out, you make another step and you say, "I am home." My true home is not in the past, not in the future. My true home is life itself—it is in the here and now. I have arrived at my true home. I feel at ease in my true home. I do not need to run anymore.

When you breathe in and say "I have arrived," if you feel that you have arrived, then smile. Smile to yourself a smile of congratulations. It is very important to arrive, because when you arrive you don't run anymore. You have stopped running. Many of us continue to run even in our sleep. We can never rest. In our dreams, in our nightmares, we continue to run. That is why we have to train ourselves to stop. Stopping helps us to be in the here and now and to touch the wonders of life for our transformation and healing. "I have arrived, I am home."

This is the first type of walking meditation. Walking slowly can be done anytime, anywhere. You may be surprised to find you will start to feel at home wherever you are, even if you are at work!

The second type of walking meditation involves walking a little more quickly. You can do this when you are walking to get somewhere, whether it is to a meeting or just across the room. You can do this when you are walking with other people, and they may not even notice.

Breathing in, you may like to take two or three steps. "I have arrived, I have arrived, I have arrived." Breathing in, I can make three steps, and I do it very naturally; people may not know that I am doing mindful walking. I enjoy every step. When you breathe out, you may like to make two or three steps: "I am home, I am home, I am home." And the energy of mindfulness inhabits and protects you.

Every time you have five or ten minutes, enjoy the practice, because it is very pleasant. Walking from one building to another, you practice mindful walking, and you enjoy every step. I always enjoy walking. I only have one style of walking: mindful walking. Even if the distance is only one or two feet, I always apply the techniques and enjoy mindful walking. Walking meditation helps me to get in touch with the wonders of life that are available in the here and now, help-ing me in my nourishment and healing so that I can be available to help those who suffer.

2 Working without Stress

Workplace Practice: Mindful Breathing

"SOMETIMES, MY JOB IS SO BUSY AND STRESSFUL,
I FEEL LIKE I AM HOLDING MY BREATH UNTIL I GET HOME."
—*Teacher, St. Paul, Minnesota*

WHEN NELSON MANDELA, the former president of South Africa, first came to France for an official visit, he was asked by the press what he would most like to do with his freedom. He said, "What would I like to do the most? Just sit down and do nothing. Because from the time I was released from prison up to now I have not had the time to just sit down and do nothing."

We would all like to have the time to sit and appreciate the stillness that comes from doing nothing. But if we were given the time, would we be able to be still and quiet? That is the problem with many of us. We complain that we don't have the time to rest, to enjoy being there. But we are used to always doing something. We have no capacity to rest and do nothing. Even if we have a rare moment of quiet at our desks, we talk on the phone or browse the internet. We are workaholics. We always need to be doing something or we think we will die. That is why learning how to be right where we are without doing anything is a very important practice, as well as a very challenging one. Mindful breathing is something we can do anywhere, whether we are sitting at our desk, standing in line, or driving.

When we get home from work, especially if we work in public service, we may notice that our bodies are full of stress and tension. Our bodies are suffering because we have not taken good care of them. We have worked them too hard. We have brought many toxins into our bodies by the way we eat, drink, work, and overwork. Mindful breathing brings the elements of peace and harmony into our breath. Whether we are lying down, sitting, or standing, the elements of stress, conflict, and tension can be released slowly through mindful breathing.

ENJOYING YOUR BREATHING

If you can find a moment to sit, wherever you are, stay there and enjoy doing nothing. Just enjoy your in-breath and out-breath. Don't allow yourself to be carried away by your thinking, worries, or projects. Just sit there and enjoy doing nothing; enjoy your breathing and the fact that you are alive and that you have twenty minutes or half an hour to enjoy doing nothing. This is very healing, transforming, and nourishing.

Of course, you don't have to do mindful breathing in a sitting position. Suppose you are standing in line waiting to copy something at work or waiting to talk with a colleague. You may be out at lunch or waiting in line to get coffee or tea. You can still practice mindful breathing and focus on enjoying yourself and the presence of people around you. Meditation can be very informal.

If you are a police officer and you are driving in a patrol car, whether you are on your way to an accident or crime scene or just patrolling, you can drive mindfully, enjoying your in-breath and out-breath. If you are a teacher or a social worker filling out reports, if you enjoy breathing in and out, if you smile, then writing the report can be very pleasant. Everything you do, if you do it mindfully, is already meditation.

OPPORTUNITIES FOR MINDFULNESS

When you eat your breakfast, even if it is just a small bite early in the morning, eat in such a way that freedom is possible. While eating breakfast, don't think of the future, of what you are going to do. Your practice is to simply eat breakfast. Your breakfast is there for you; you have to be there for your breakfast. You can chew each morsel of food with joy and freedom.

When I hold a piece of bread, I look at it, and sometimes I smile at it. The piece of bread is an ambassador of the cosmos offering nourishment and support. Looking deeply into the piece of bread, I see the sunshine, the clouds, the great Earth. Without the sunshine, no wheat can grow. Without the clouds, there is no rain for the wheat to grow. Without the great Earth, nothing can grow. That is why the piece of bread that I hold in my hand is a wonder of life. It is there for all of us. We have to be there for it.

Eat with gratitude. And when you put the piece of bread into your mouth, chew only your bread and not your projects, worries, fears, or anger. This is the practice of mindfulness. You chew mindfully and you know that you are chewing the bread, the wonderful nourishment of life. This brings you freedom and joy. Eat every morsel of your breakfast like that, not allowing yourself to be carried away from the experience of eating. This is a training.

When you brush your teeth, how much time can you afford for brushing your teeth? At least one minute, maybe two? Brush your teeth in such a way that freedom and joy are possible, not allowing yourself to be carried away by concerns about what you will do after you are done. "I am standing here, brushing my teeth. I still have teeth to brush. I have toothpaste, a toothbrush. And my practice is to be alive, to be free to enjoy tooth-brushing." Don't allow yourself to be a slave of the past or the future. This practice is the practice of freedom. And if freedom is there, you will enjoy brushing your teeth. Resist the tendency to be carried away by your thoughts and fears.

Whatever else you do at work, you probably use the restroom. It's interesting that in the United States you call it the restroom; do you feel restful in your restroom? In France, they used to call it *la cabine d'aisance*. "Aisance" means ease; you feel at ease, you feel comfortable. So when you go to the restroom, feel at ease with it, enjoy your time in the restroom. That's my practice. When I urinate, I allow myself to be entirely with the act of urinating. If you have freedom, then urinating is very pleasant. You allow yourself to invest one hundred percent of your body and mind into the act of urinating. It can free you. It can be joyful. If you have experienced a urinary tract infection, you know that urinating can be painful. You don't have any infection, therefore urinating is very pleasant, restful. Be free during the thirty seconds or one minute of urinating.

When you drive to and from work, instead of thinking of your destination, enjoy every moment of driving. Before I begin my work of teaching, I do not bother myself with the question: "What will my friends ask and how shall I answer?" I do not bother myself with this question at all. From my room to the place where I teach, I enjoy every step and I live each moment of my walk deeply. When I arrive, I feel fresh and ready to offer my answers to questions. It is possible to enjoy mindful living during every moment of daily life.

Breathing in, I am aware of my in-breath. Breathing out,
I am aware of my out-breath. Breathing in, I am aware of my body.
Breathing out, I release the tension in my body.

When you breathe in, if you bring your full attention to your in-breath, you become your in-breath. It is because you are mindful of your in-breath and concentrated on it that you and your in-breath become one. Don't think that this is something difficult or tiring to do. Breathing in may be very enjoyable. When you breathe in, you can appreciate the fact that you are still alive. Breath is the essence of life; without breath, we are nothing but a dead body. To be aware of your vitality through breathing can bring immense joy. If you are used to the practice, this awareness is present whenever you breathe. You don't have to force the breath. You allow yourself to breathe in naturally. Don't try to struggle with your in-breath. Just allow it to be the way it is. Whether it is short or long, harmonious or not harmonious, you allow it to be that way. You just become aware of it. You are like a flower that need not do anything in order for the sun to bathe it in warmth.

Breathing in, I'm aware of my in-breath. Breathing out, I'm aware of my out-breath. Don't interfere. Just become aware of it. And during the time you become aware of your in-breath and out-breath, you naturally stop your thinking. Stopping your thoughts is very helpful. If you are caught in your thinking all the time, you get tired and are not capable of being present. The philosopher René Descartes said: "I think, therefore I am." But I don't agree: "I think, therefore I am not there. I am not really there to touch the wonders of life." You can naturally stop your thoughts if you focus your attention fully on your in-breath and your out-breath. After one or two minutes of practice, the quality of your in-breath and out-breath will improve. Your breath will become deeper, slower, and more harmonious and peaceful, whether you are lying down, sitting, or walking. By practicing mindful breathing, we bring the elements of harmony and peace into our bodies.

Breathing in, I am aware of my heart.
Breathing out, I smile to my heart.

This is the practice of mindfulness. It is a practice of peace, of reconciliation. When we bring our attention to our heart, we realize that our heart is wonderful. The proper functioning of our heart is one of the basic conditions of our well-being. There are those of us who do not have a normal heart, those who might be subject to a heart attack at any time. Their deepest desire is to have a normal heart. By breathing mindfully, you bring your attention to your heart, and that attention has a healing effect.

It is easy for us to neglect our heart. In our life, we may have abused alcohol or cigarettes. We may have given our heart a difficult time. Your heart is essential for your well-being. So go home to your heart. Embrace it tenderly with the energy of mindfulness.

Going home to our hearts is very comforting. Maybe this is the first time you've gone back to your heart with loving kindness and compassion. Breathing in and becoming aware of your heart is an act of friendship, of enlightenment. Once you are in touch with your heart, you will know exactly what to do, and especially what not to do, in order to really care for it.

This practice is very concrete and clear. We can do it at work,

૭ई

alone or in groups, supporting each other. It allows you to see deeply into the here and now and to get in touch with the wonders of life so that you will be strong and lucid enough to handle the difficult situations you encounter at work.

3 Transforming Anger

Workplace Practic: Mindful Consumption

"EVERYDAY, I SEE ANGRY PEOPLE AND THEY ARE IN SO MUCH PAIN.
IT'S EVERYWHERE. AND AS A THERAPIST, I'M IN THE LINE OF FIRE.
A LOT OF IT IS DIRECTED AT ME."
—*Therapist, New York, New York*

SAY YOU ARE a police officer and you have to stop a car and see whether someone in it is carrying a gun. To do this well, you need mindfulness. For you know that not every car holds a criminal. Suppose you begin looking for the goodness in people when you pull them over. If you are truly mindful, you will see both the positive things and the negative things in everything. This is hard when you are at work. But if you begin with yourself, when you are at home or alone, and get to know your own anger through practicing mindfulness, then it becomes easier when you are in a stressful situation with other people.

Every ordinary act can be transformed into an act of mindfulness. When you breathe mindfully, this is mindfulness of breathing. When you walk mindfully, this is mindfulness of walking. When you look at things mindfully, whether it is the blue sky or the beautiful trees, it's called mindfulness of looking.

If mindfulness were to focus only on the negative things, that would be a pity. Right mindfulness has the capacity to transform the negative things. Of course, mindfulness is not only mindfulness of the positive. When anger manifests, we practice mindfulness of anger. But the practice of transformation occurs every time anger manifests, and we take good care of it, treating it with mindfulness and compassion.

TAKING CARE OF OUR ANGER

Anger has the power to burn and destroy. If you don't know the practice of mindfulness, you will allow yourself to be burned and destroyed by anger. You will suffer and those around you will suffer as well. That is why, when you notice that anger is coming up, you have to do something right away. It is important to act, rather than react. You have to act by inviting the seed of mindfulness to arise. We breathe in and we breathe out, making steps, generating the energy of mindfulness in order to take care of our anger.

Suppose a mother is working in the living room and she hears her baby crying. Chances are she puts down whatever she is doing and goes to her baby's room. She picks up the baby and holds it tenderly in her arms. This is exactly what we can do when the energy of anger comes up. Our anger is our ailing baby. We must nurture it in order to calm it.

The practitioner knows that her anger is not her enemy; her anger is her suffering baby. She must take good care of her baby, using the energy of mindfulness to embrace her anger in the most tender way. She can say: "Breathing in, I know that anger is in me. Breathing out, I am peacefully holding my anger."

When we breathe like this, there are two kinds of energy: the energy of anger and the energy of mindfulness. The energy of mindfulness continues to be generated by the practice of mindful breathing and mindful walking, and it begins to penetrate into the zone of the angry energy. In summer, if you go into a room that is too hot, hopefully you can open a window or turn on a fan or the air conditioner. The cool air does not need to chase the hot air out. Instead, the coolness comes and tenderly embraces the heat. And fifteen minutes later, the air is different.

So it is with bringing mindfulness to our anger. There is no fighting in this practice. Your anger is not your enemy; it's you. It's not good to do violence to yourself. Don't say that mindfulness is good and anger is evil, and good has to fight evil. In this tradition of mindfulness, there is no battle to be won.

Suppose we are feeling a very deep anger that will not go away. We have to be very patient. By continuing to generate the energy of mindfulness and tenderly embrace our anger, we will find some relief. But we can do more. With mindfulness and concentration, we can also look deeply into the nature of our anger and find its roots. This is called mindfulness of consumption.

In order to forget that we have blocks of pain, sorrow, fear, and violence, we lose ourselves in the practice of consumption. Why do we turn on the television? Why do we continue to watch, even if the programs are not interesting at all? We watch because we want something to cover up our pain, sorrow, fear, and anger. We don't want those feelings to come up, so we suppress them by consuming. There is some feeling of loneliness, fear, or depression inside that we don't want, so we pick up the newspaper, we turn on the radio, we turn on the television, we pick up the phone, we go for a drive. We do everything we can to avoid confronting our true selves. This kind of consumption is a practice of running away, and the items we consume continue to bring the toxins of violence, fear, and anger into us. By practicing an embargo on our negative feelings, we create a situation of bad circulation in our psyche, suppressing our unwanted thought patterns and not allowing them to circulate. When we create a situation of bad circulation in our consciousness, it causes symptoms of depression and mental illness.

When the blood in our body does not circulate well, we experience physical pain—we have a headache, a backache, sometimes there is pain everywhere. When we exercise and massage to help the blood circulate well, we diminish these symptoms in our body. The same is true with our consciousness. If we block unpleasant thought patterns through consumption, we create bad circulation in our psyche, and symptoms of mental illness will appear. That is why it's very important to lift the embargo, allowing fear, pain, and sorrow to come up. You can only do this if you are ready, or you'll be overwhelmed by your suffering. You invite the negative thoughts to come up with the energy of mindfulness generated by your practice. This energy is there to recognize, embrace, and transform. If you practice, if you know how to sit, then the energy of mindfulness and concentration within you will be powerful enough to do the work of recognizing, embracing, and bringing relief to your suffering. After being embraced by mindfulness and finding relief, the energy of fear, anger, and depression that were growing within you will lose some of their power.

WATERING OUR SEEDS

In Buddhist psychology, we speak of consciousness in terms of seeds, like a seed of corn. There are many kinds of seeds that lie deep in our consciousness: seeds of anger, violence, fear, jealousy, despair, discrimination, and hate. They are all there. When they sleep they are okay. But if someone comes along and waters these seeds they will manifest as energy and they will make us suffer. We also have wholesome seeds in us, namely seeds of understanding, awakening, compassion, nonviolence, nondiscrimination, joy, and forgiveness. If you do not live in a good environment, these wholesome seeds will have no chance to be watered. That is why it is very important to select an environment where the wholesome seeds in us can be watered every day, and the negative seeds will rarely be watered.

You can see it as a bath of mindfulness, where the energy of anger, depression, and fear washes away. When that negative energy is being fed by our experience of suffering, then it can grow. But when we bathe in mindfulness, we provide our negative energy with a different kind of nourishment. The nourishment of mindfulness will weaken anger, depression, and fear, and send them back to their places in the store consciousness as seeds. When they manifest again, we will give them the same kind of mindfulness bath. We are no longer afraid of the blocks of suffering in us, because now we know how to handle them. We can say: "My dear old friends, you are welcome to come up. I will offer you a bath of mindfulness so you will feel better." When they are free to circulate, then the symptoms of mental illness begin to disappear. Those of you who are in the field of psychotherapy already know this. We have to apply the techniques to ourselves in the workplace before we can help people at work.

How do we handle the fear, sorrow, anger, depression, and violence within us? This is a very important thing to learn. Parents must learn how to do it if they truly want to love their children. And in doing so, they teach their children how to do it. Teachers must know how to do this in order to set an example for their students. Psychotherapists and psychologists must learn how to do it in order to set an example for their patients. Doctors and nurses must be able to do this before they can help their patients. And I believe that law enforcement officers need to be able to handle their loneliness, suffering, and anger before they can truly help the people in custody, in school, and in prison. Because those people are there to be helped and not to be punished.

MINDFUL CONSUMPTION

Suppose you are a corrections officer and you have to do your work from midnight until seven in the morning, while your family, your loved ones, and the other officers are asleep. The work can be very lonely, painful, depressing. If you know the practice you will be able to transform the seven hours of your work into a positive experience. Otherwise, you will suffer during your shift. You may ask: "Why do I have to be here at this time when everyone is sleeping? Why do I have to suffer alone?" Suddenly you become very unhappy. You don't see your future. You're overwhelmed by loneliness and fear. You may begin to sweat, to tremble, and you don't know why. You imagine that a revolt in the prison would change your situation—you would have to do something to respond to what was happening. If the seed of fear comes up, your adrenaline is pumping, then you can escape the persistent boredom and depression that might otherwise be with you through your shift.

Long hours of being a guard or officer can be very destructive, frightening, and unhealthy. When you go home, everyone wakes up to be with you, to eat breakfast and get ready to go to work or school. They begin their day and you go to sleep. You may sleep most of the day. You may spend the rest of the day just watching television. And the kind of television you watch can bring more depression, anger, violence, and craving into you. Then you eat your dinner; maybe you eat alone. Maybe you sleep again. And when the time is close, you have to drag yourself out of bed to get ready to go and take your responsibility from midnight to seven o'clock. This kind of living may become very difficult. If you continue, you may find yourself feeling depleted and angry all the time, feeling like your spirit is malnourished. This can take a toll on your family and personal life.

Your depression and anger are like a hungry belly rumbling for food. Nothing can survive without food. You will see that you must nourish and feed your love with the appropriate food, or your love will turn to hatred. If you look deeply into the nature of your anger and identify the source of nutriment that you have used to feed it, you are already on the path of freedom.

If we notice that we are blocked by fear, anger, and despair, it is because we have constantly fed these seeds within us. To stop feeding them is our practice. If we don't stop feeding them and we only try to deal with the symptoms when they arise, we won't go very far. That is why mindfulness of consumption is very important. It has to go hand-in-hand with the practice of transformation.

We have spoken about getting in touch with the positive, healing, and nourishing elements, and not just allowing ourselves to be penetrated by the negative things. How many hours, how many scenes of violence do our children witness by watching television? By the time they are twelve years old, they may have watched many thousands of scenes of murder and violence, and all of that is preserved in their consciousness. If our children consume three hours of television a day, this may be because they don't have any other source of joy. They may not be able to enjoy sitting close to you and talking to you, because communication has become difficult between you and your children, and for that reason it's not a pleasure for them to sit close to you and converse. They may be covering up that kind of sadness and loneliness with television. There are many television programs that encourage craving, anger, and violence. By feeding your children television instead of closeness and conversation, you are allowing this violence to come into the collective consciousness of the organism of your family.

We feel lonely. We feel alone. We feel sick. We want to forget our loneliness by consuming. We consume newspapers, magazines, and television. We destroy ourselves through consumption. Meanwhile, the companies that are creating these products are getting richer and richer by feeding their products to you.

Some people feel that consuming mindfully, and encouraging corporations to create more mindful material, somehow limits our freedom. But freedom should be understood in such a way that it can protect us, our family, and society. We are not free to kill. We are not free to poison people with toxic products. We have to be responsible for our society. If we feel that we are free to produce the kind of items that bring a lot of toxins, violence, and craving into the body and consciousness of the people, especially of the younger generation, then we are destroying our collective body and consciousness, and we are destroying the future. We act on the basis of our cravings. We want power, wealth, and fame. These desires can cause us to neglect our responsibility to sustain the well-being of our communities. That is why true freedom has to go hand-in-hand with responsibility. We have a statue of liberty on the East Coast. We must build a statue of responsibility on the West Coast. These two elements do not contradict each other. It is our sense of responsibility that will protect us and protect our freedom.

~§ Workplace Practice: Mindful Consumption

The Buddha talks about four kinds of food we consume every day, called the four nutriments. We can be mindful of what we ingest both at work and at home. Transforming our consumption can also transform our anger and what we express to the world.

The first nutriment is what we consume as edible food. If we don't eat mindfully, we bring a lot of toxins and conflict into our body. The way we grow our food and the way we raise our livestock is often very violent. We destroy a lot of land and pollute a lot of water just to make meat, and then the meat we eat contains all of that anger and violence. If we look deeply, we see that we have caused a lot of suffering around us just in the way we eat and consume. The United Nations Hunger Project estimates that about 20,000 people die every day from hunger or hunger-related causes. Three-fourths of these deaths are children under the age of five. To produce a piece of meat, you must use a lot of grain. When we eat that meat, we are eating the flesh of our own sons and daughters. Who are the 20,000 people who die every day? If they are not our children, whose are they?

As a monk, I don't eat meat, I don't drink alcohol, and I don't smoke. It is not a hardship and it keeps my body healthy. Those of you working in public service—as corrections officers, teachers, or health workers—you may also decide to practice in this way. Your way of eating and consuming is your way of teaching other people. We should eat in such a way that others have a chance to live and our children have a future. This is possible; and we don't have to suffer at all by choosing to eat mindfully. In fact, we will bring ourselves a lot of joy, compassion, and understanding: the foundation of true happiness.

The second kind of nutriment the Buddha talks about is sensory impression. What we hear, see, feel, and think are foods we consume through our senses. To illustrate sensory impression, the Buddha used the image of a cow who has a skin disease. Her skin is missing in places, so wherever she goes, whether in water, on the ground, near a wall or a tree, creatures come to feed on her flesh. She has no protection. We are like that cow. If we do not practice mindfulness, then we will be assaulted by what we take in through our six sense organs: our eyes, ears, nose, tongue, body, and consciousness. There is so much violence, hatred, and anger around us. If we allow ourselves to consume it, we ourselves become violent and fearful.

When you drive through the city, you automatically consume. There are advertisements, there are noises; you have no choice but to consume. When you watch television, you consume. When you read the newspaper, you consume. When you listen to music, you consume. And the items of your consumption may bring poisons, war, and depression into your body and your consciousness.

If you and your loved ones consume in a way that brings craving, violence, and hatred into your consciousness and the collective consciousness of those you care about, then you are allowing a virus to come into your body and your community.

Just listening to a conversation full of hatred, fear, and pessimism is a form of consumption. It brings these elements into your consciousness, which can be very toxic. When you listen to negative words, anger, fear, and confusion come into you. You have to protect yourself. You should be able to say: "I have heard enough of that. Let us talk about something else."

The third nutriment that the Buddha spoke of is volition. Volition is your inner motivation, your deepest desire, the thing that drives you. Every one of us has a deepest desire. We must identify it, and

❦

call it by its true name. Perhaps your desire is to help other people, and that is why you entered public service. Or perhaps your desire is something else entirely, and you find yourself doing public service work but wishing you were doing something different. The Buddha had a desire; he wanted to transform all his suffering. He wanted to be enlightened in order to be able to help other people. He did not believe that by being a politician he could help many people; that is why he chose the way of a monk.

There are those of us who believe that happiness is only possible when we gain a lot of money, fame, power, and sex. That kind of desire belongs to the third category of food spoken of by the Buddha. The Buddha offered this image to illustrate his teaching: There is a young man who loves to be alive—he doesn't want to die. In fact, he will do anything to preserve his own life, including harming and killing others. There are two very strong men who wish to take revenge on this man who clings so violently to his own life. They drag him to a pit of burning coals and try to throw him into the glowing embers so he will die. He resists, but in the end he is too weak to struggle against their strength. The Buddha said, "Your deepest desire will bring you either to happiness or to hell. "

Craving, whether for wealth, sex, power, or fame, can lead you to suffering. But if you have a healthy desire—like the desire to protect life, to protect the environment, or to help people, while still taking the time to take care of yourself, and to love and take care of your loved ones—this is the kind of desire that will bring you to happiness.

Perhaps in your work you have seen others hurt and you wish to seek revenge. There are people everywhere in the world whose deepest desire is vengeance. When hatred and vengeance are our deepest

ৼৄ

desires, we suffer terribly. We are like the young man dragged into the pit of glowing embers. Our deepest desire should be to love and to help, not to seek revenge, to punish, or to kill.

At work, we can remember our true volition, which is not power or revenge. If we practice being calm and focused, and water the seeds of wisdom and compassion in us, then we are learning the art of mindful consumption and we will find our true volition.

The fourth nutriment the Buddha speaks of is consciousness. When fear, anger, or pain enter our consciousness, mindfulness is there to bring relief. It would be better if anger, fear, and despair would not show up on the upper level of our consciousness. Life would be more pleasant. But because we nurture them every day and we ingest the toxins of violence, fear, and anger every day, these seeds have become very strong in us, and they push open the door of mind consciousness and settle themselves there.

Our subconsciousness is like a basement. Anything we don't want, we store down there. We can call it the "store consciousness." Everything beautiful that we like, we display in our living room, which is the "mind consciousness." It's not pleasant to have the things we don't want—our despair, anger, and pain—on display in the living room. That is why we practice a kind of embargo. We lock the door. We don't want the fear, pain, and anger to come up. We tend to fill up the living room with guests, leaving no room for the things in the basement to come up. That is the practice for the majority in our society. It's not pleasant to allow the pain, the sorrow, and the fear to come up. Our policy as individuals, and the policy of our government are very much alike: to ignore the real suffering within, to have our mind preoccupied with other issues, so that we forget to deal with the real roots of our suffering.

❧

There are a number of things we can do. First of all, we have to change our way of thinking. If we feel that we are victims of a situation, then we cannot overcome it. We can practice mindfulness in such a way that our time becomes meaningful, nourishing, and healing. We can live each twenty-four hours in such a way that understanding and compassion can be cultivated. Without understanding and compassion, happiness and joy will not be possible.

Suppose, as a guard or a corrections officer, you try to look at the inmates and understand their suffering and despair. You practice looking deeply to see how these people have arrived here to spend their time like this. They are making each other suffer. They inflict suffering on each other out of ignorance, anger, and hatred. They are locked in prison; unable to go out and do the things they enjoy. They suffer enough as it is. But because they don't know how to handle their suffering, they inflict suffering on the other inmates, making the situation worse. Hell is created through this kind of practice.

Even those of us who are not in prison, who see ourselves as so different from these prisoners, suffer in the same way. But we can transform our suffering by being conscious of our joy. Being mindful of our joy helps it to grow. Suppose we are standing as a group, facing a glorious sunset. Mindfulness helps us to be free from the past and free from the future so that we can get in touch with the tools we possess for our transformation and healing.

There are times when we have to think about our past or our future. But there are times when we can afford to focus our attention fully on the beautiful, refreshing, and healing things. When your shift is over and you go home, who is it that forbids you to enjoy walking meditation, touching the beauty around you, listening to the birds, and contemplating the blue sky or the stars?

You may want to keep a list of the four nutriments with you at work. It may help remind you what you are choosing to consume and what is consuming you. Mindfulness is always helpful, whether the object of mindfulness is positive or negative. When we embrace anger and fear with mindfulness, we can penetrate those emotions with tenderness, attention, and care, giving them a chance to be transformed. Mindfulness carries with it the energy of concentration, and wherever there is mindfulness and concentration, there is insight. If you live your life mindfully, with concentration, you live every moment of your life deeply, and you begin to focus on what is occurring in the present moment. Insight is the outcome, the flower that blooms on the ground of mindfulness and concentration. Insight is what can liberate you. If you have insight, then even in prison, you are free.

SECTION 2

∼§ Peace in Our Work Environment

4 Nourishing a Healthy Work Environment

Workplace Practice: Watering Seeds

"WHAT'S THE HARDEST THING ABOUT BEING A COP?
I KNOW THAT PEOPLE ARE EXPECTING ME TO SAY: IT'S THE
DANGER, NOT KNOWING IF I'M GOING TO COME HOME AT NIGHT.
I KNOW SOME PEOPLE ARE THINKING IT'S THE VIOLENCE;
IT'S THE ANGER THAT YOU SEE ON A DAILY BASIS. IT'S NONE OF
THOSE THINGS. THE HARDEST THING FOR ME IS WHEN I SEE
CHILDREN WHO ARE OUT OF CONTROL AND THE PARENTS
WHO DON'T KNOW WHAT TO DO, OR I SEE CHILDREN WHO
ARE LIVING IN A VIOLENT AND VERY UNHEALTHY ENVIRONMENT
AND I DON'T KNOW WHAT TO DO."
—*A Police Officer, Madison, Wisconsin*

THE PRACTICES we have talked about so far—mindful walking, mindful breathing, and mindful consumption—are practices that you can do on your own, both at home and at work. These individual private practices are the base, the seat, of your personal transformation. You may engage in these mindfulness practices no matter what the environment is around you. But it is also helpful to think about how to change your environment.

Many years ago, during the Vietnam War, I sat in a vacant airfield in the highlands of Vietnam waiting for a plane to travel north. There had been a great flood there and I was hoping to help bring relief to the victims. Because the situation was urgent, I had boarded a military plane that let me off in the highlands of Plei Ku. I was there waiting for the next plane when an American officer, who was also waiting for the plane, came and sat near me. There were only the two of us at the airfield. I looked at this young officer with a lot of compassion. Why did he have to come here to kill or to be killed? Speaking only out of compassion, I said to him: "You must be very afraid of the Vietcong," (the North Vietnamese Army). But I was not skillful. Instead of him seeing me as a friend, I had watered the seed of fear in him, and he suddenly touched his gun and asked me: "Are you Vietcong?"

Before coming to Vietnam, U.S. Army officers were told that everyone in Vietnam could be a communist guerrilla, and fear inhabited every American soldier. The soldiers had been taught that every child and every monk could be a guerrilla agent and they saw enemies everywhere. I had tried to express my sympathy to him, but as soon as he heard the word "Vietcong," his fear overwhelmed him and he reached for his gun.

I breathed in and out and then I said, very calmly, "I am not Vietcong. I am waiting for my plane to go to Da Nang and help the people hurt by the flooding there." By sitting very still and speaking calmly, I could express the sympathy I had for him and the soldier was able to feel it. He took his hand off his gun.

The war had created a lot of victims, Americans as well as Vietnamese. If I had acted out of fear, he would have shot me out of his own fear. Dangers don't just come from outside. They also come from inside us. If you are not serene and solid enough, if you are not lucid and calm enough, you draw dangers and accidents to you.

The quality and the happiness of a human being depend on the quality of the seeds they have in their store consciousness. We should organize our life in such a way that the wholesome seeds in us have a chance to be watered every day. This is a crucial practice. Our society cannot get out of this situation of violence and despair without this kind of practice. We need to protect ourselves with a good environment, because we are exposed to negative watering every day. Often, both at work and at home, what we see, what we hear, and what we read water the seeds of violence, despair, and hatred in us and in our children.

The practice of transformation and healing cannot be effective without the practice of seeking or creating a sane environment. When someone is sick, we have to bring him to a place where he can be treated and heal. Suppose someone has eaten or drunk something that has given him diarrhea. The first thing is to advise that person to stop eating or drinking that thing, and instead to eat and drink the things that will bring healing. Maybe some medicine is needed. But what is important is to prevent that person from continuing to eat and drink the things that will worsen the situation. It's the same with consciousness. If someone is affected by the poisons of violence, anger, and despair, and we want to help her heal, we have to bring her out of the situation where she continues to ingest the toxins of violence and fear. This is very simple, very clear. This is not only the job of educators. Everyone has to participate in creating safe environments for ourselves and our children.

✍ Workplace Practice: Watering Seeds

Suppose you have a partner or colleague at work, and you want to make sure this relationship goes well. There are two things you may like to do. The first thing is to make a commitment to the other person. You may say: "Partner, I want you to be happy and not to suffer. And I know you want the same thing for me. You know that I have the seeds of anger and jealousy in me. If you care about me, please be careful not to water these seeds in me. If you do, my jealousy and anger will manifest, and I will suffer and cause you to suffer. I promise the same thing. I will not do anything to water the seeds of anger and jealousy in myself. I also promise not to water the seeds of anger and jealousy in you."

As colleagues at work, we have to protect each other. This means that we recognize the seed of suffering in all of us, and we make the vow not to water that seed in our everyday lives. Instead, we should speak aloud of the positive qualities in our colleague. This is called the practice of positive watering. We may say, "I know that you have the seeds of compassion, joy, and forgiveness. I make the vow to try to water these seeds every day. It's not only for your sake, but also for my sake. I also promise that I will water the same beautiful seeds in me by reading, by listening, and by touching the things that can water these good seeds in me. Together we protect each other." This practice will transform the relationship in just a few days.

The second thing you and your colleague can do is to seek the kind of environment where the good seeds have a chance to be watered. This is extremely important. If you are a sociologist, if you are a psychologist, if you are a doctor, a teacher, an officer, or a parent, you try your best to relieve the suffering of the people you care about. But if those people continue to ingest toxins, then what you are doing will not mean much. You are trying to alleviate symptoms, but the roots of the problem are always there.

You may work every day in an environment that has these toxins in it. How can you change this work environment so that it includes reminders of the positive seeds in each person? Small things may make a big difference. What do you and your colleagues eat during the day? What do you look at on the wall? What sounds do you listen to? If you can change even one of these things, so that at least once a day you and your colleagues are consuming something beautiful instead of just toxins, it will transform your work environment and your relationships with your colleagues.

5 Collective Resources

Workplace Practice: The Second Body System

"MY FATHER WAS A POLICE OFFICER. HE NEVER TALKED
ABOUT HIS WORK. HE PASSED AWAY WHEN I WAS THIRTEEN,
SO I DIDN'T KNOW WHAT HIS JOB WAS LIKE. IT DIDN'T EVEN
OCCUR TO ME WHAT HE HAD TO FEEL AND EXPERIENCE."
—*Doctor, San Francisco, California*

SOME YEARS AGO, a young American businessman came to Plum
Village, the retreat community where I live and practice in southern
France. He was very happy there, because he had a strong community around him and he was supported by the presence of other prac-
titioners of mindfulness. Because of this, he was able to be in the
present and notice the wonders of life all around him.

One day he went to the market to do some shopping. In the mar-
ketplace, without the community around him, he started rushing. He
tried to do everything quickly so that he could return to Plum Village.
During the previous three weeks, he had not rushed anywhere. The
collective energy of mindfulness in the community was strong
enough to keep him in the present moment, not trying to speed to the
next. But alone in the market, he noticed that he wanted to do everything quickly in order to get back quickly.

Because he had been practicing mindfulness for those three weeks, he was able to recognize that he wanted to rush and he even had an insight about where that need to rush came from. He remembered that his mother was always rushing, unable to stop. When he recognized what he was doing and where his rushing energy came from, he breathed in and out and recognized the part of his mother that was in him. Suddenly the need to rush disappeared. It simply went away. He continued shopping, breathing mindfully the whole time, without ever having another urge to rush.

Even if you are alone, you still have to practice in order to protect yourself. In law enforcement, teaching, and other public service occupations, this means not just protecting yourself from violence and accidents that come from outside, but also protecting yourself from accidents that come from inside you. If you spill something, trip, or blow up in anger at someone, these are all accidents that come from not practicing mindfulness inside yourself. If you are peaceful and lucid, you will not draw accidents to you.

ROCKS IN THE RIVER

If you are surrounded by people who practice mindfulness together, then you will be supported by the collective energy, and the practice will become very easy and natural. We all have pain, sorrow, and fear within. Don't keep it for yourself. None of us are strong enough to embrace our pain and sorrow alone. Allow the community to embrace it for you.

When you throw a rock into the river, no matter how small the rock is, it will sink. But if you have a boat, you can carry many tons of rocks and you won't sink. The same is true of our sorrow, fear, and pain. If we allow the collective energy of mindfulness to embrace us, then we will not sink in the ocean of suffering. We can practice alone, yes, but it is much more wonderful to have a community to practice mindfulness with. When many people practice mindfulness together, the collective energy is strong enough to help us do the work of transformation and healing. Without this collective energy, we are likely to lose sight of our practice and abandon it after a few months. If you want your practice to continue, create a group of people around you who practice together, and your practice will be sustained by the collective energy of the group.

Ask someone to go for a walk with you or just to sit quietly with you for a few minutes. This may be difficult or embarassing at first, but you will find it is worth it. Even if one other person, a second body, is being mindful, you will find you have created a small oasis of safety and mindfulness. Even if you cannot, at first, find others to practice with you, start practicing mindfulness by yourself. People are practicing all over the world. You are not alone. Every one of us is capable of contributing to the collective energy of mindfulness. Your practice of mindful breathing and mindful walking is supporting all of us. We each do our best to contribute. When we practice mindful breathing and mindful walking, then we become the bell of mindfulness for everyone. When you walk mindfully, enjoying every step you make, you remind others to do the same, even if they do not know what you are doing. When you smile, you smile in support of all of us and you remind all of us to do the same. So your practice is very important.

✥ Workplace Practice: The Second Body System

We have to organize our day in an intelligent way in order to protect ourselves. The easiest way to do this is, again, to create a community that has similar goals and ideas. In Plum Village, we have a practice called the Second Body System. Every one of us has another person whom we take care of beside ourselves. We call this other person our Second Body. We care for this other person and are aware of what is going on with them.

Perhaps, if you are in law enforcement, you already have a "partner" who is like this for you. If not, it is worth finding one, even if it is not official. If you are a teacher or a social worker, perhaps there is another teacher or colleague whom you can start doing this with. It is possible to discuss with your colleagues how to reorganize your day so that everybody can profit from the collective energy of mindfulness, concentration, and joy.

With your Second Body, you know whether or not that person is happy or has a problem. You know when your Second Body needs help. And someone else is looking out for you in the same way. Each person in the community or workplace can be the Second Body for someone else, and in turn be looked after by someone else as *their* Second Body. A Second Body system is like a chain, one person caring for another.

With the Second Body System, we always feel supported by our community through the person who acts as our Second Body. As nurses, as doctors, psychologists, or police officers, it is possible to organize our work life like that. In this way, we can combine our energy of mindfulness and not feel so alone. When the energy of mindfulness is being generated in our community, our family, our agency, and our departments, we no longer need to solve our problems by ourselves.

6 Companionship and Community

Workplace Practice: Beginning Anew in the Workplace

"As police officers, many of us have families that
we come home to. But when that work pager goes off,
whether it's a holiday, whether it's a birthday party,
or whether it's the middle of the night, I have to say
good-bye to my family and come take care of your family."
—*Police Officer, Madison, Wisconsin*

THERE ARE POLICE OFFICERS who know they can survive as
an officer on the street because of the training and skills they acquire
through daily experience, but they cannot handle going back to the
police station. There is misunderstanding, jealousy, and anger in the
community of police officers. Sometimes officers accuse each other of
betraying the department. Sometimes officers, like all of us, don't
help each other. They don't understand each other as a community,
as a family. When we are not able to recognize and embrace each
other's pain, we cannot help it to transform. This keeps us from mov-
ing forward in our path of service.

A community requires that everyone have a chance to speak and
be heard. Imagine if officers learned to communicate well with each
other and think of the department as a community. It is important
not to use authority as the tool to get things done at work. Police

officers should not only give orders. Work should be organized in such a way that every individual working in the department becomes a member of an organism where mutual understanding is possible. Working together, as a sisterhood and brotherhood, everyone will be stronger, more solid, and more prepared to cope with the difficulties outside.

In the monastic community I live in, no one has a private bank account. No one has an individual car. Even our clothes belong to the community. As you gain more experience in the monastic community and become a big sister or big brother, then a newly ordained brother or sister will use your robe. Sisterhood and brotherhood are what sustain us and help us to be happy in our daily life.

The same thing is true with police officers, corrections officers, schoolteachers, psychotherapists, and people in all professions. We have to build up our community to sustain, protect, and nourish us. We each have our own talents. One teacher may be good at interacting with the children, but have a hard time planning lessons. One police officer may be very skilled at saving people's lives, but less skilled in writing reports. There are those who are good at paperwork. There are those who are good at dealing with difficult situations. As a principal, an officer, a boss, a lieutenant, or a captain, your job is to encourage and praise people's strengths and to help them with their difficulties. These kinds of small things build up understanding, friendship, and brotherhood that will sustain every member of the community. This is what we do in our community of practice and it can be done in the workplace as well.

The first step each of us must take if we want to create this community is to bring attention to ourselves and notice what is going on in our bodies and with our emotions. What kind of suffering and pain do we have in us? We need to come home to ourselves in order to take care of our pain, sorrow, and violence. The first step is to see the path, even if you have not transformed all of your suffering, fear, and pain. Even if you have transformed only one or two percent of the suffering in you, you can be happy because you have now seen a path.

The second step is to work with your family and those closest to you. You don't need to wait until you have transformed all of your suffering to help your family. This is the second step. Use loving speech and listen deeply in communication with your parents, your partner, and your children. Persuade them to join you on the path of transformation and healing, because your family should be the foundation of support for your practice. Without the support of your family, your partner, your children, it is more difficult to be mindful yourself.

Can your family come home to itself? Together, you can see whether there is enough harmony, communication, understanding, and love in the family. Together, you can look at any violence and division in the family and learn how to handle these blocks of suffering. This is crucial for rebuilding oneself and rebuilding the family.

There are families where nobody feels that it is a real family. It is like a hotel where people simply go to sleep; everyone has his own life and there is no communication, no mutual support. The practice of returning home to ourselves is used to rebuild the family and turn it into an organism. When there is enough awareness, transformation, and joy in the family, you and your family will become a source of support in your community.

The third step is to transform yourself to help your community. Your community may be your colleagues in the workplace. If you are teachers, you can organize as a community of teachers. Every school and university has an administration. If you want to serve your students, to help them in the path of transformation, healing and love, then you have to improve the quality of the administration, the faculty, the board of trustees. If there is division, if there is hatred, if there is competition for power, then you cannot serve yourself, you cannot be happy, and you cannot serve your students.

The same thing is true within a hospital or a prison. If the doctors, the nurses, and the administration of the hospital hate each other and do not communicate, the patients will suffer. If you are a corrections officer, you have to bring the practice first to your colleagues or everyone will suffer. Wherever you work, think of your colleagues as your brothers and sisters. Your workplace is your community every day.

No matter how high your rank, behave as a big brother or a big sister to others, and transform your community of service into a real community. This is possible. If there is division, hatred, and fear in the community, then you cannot be nourished. You will not have joy and stability enough to go out and serve. You will bring the suffering back to your home, to your family, and to yourself.

To help your agency, your administration, and your community to go back to itself, you have to acknowledge that division, hatred, jealousy, and lack of communication exist. You have to sit together and speak to each other about how to reduce the negativity within your department. There is a concrete technique for doing this called "Beginning Anew." If you apply this technique, you will notice changes within just a few weeks. As a lifelong community-builder, I have seen this many times.

≈§ Workplace Practice: Beginning Anew

In my community at Plum Village, we have a weekly session called "Beginning Anew," which everyone attends. The practice is to share, to create an atmosphere of brotherhood and sisterhood, to make communication possible, and to give everyone a chance to speak out. We use deep, compassionate listening and gentle, loving speech. Everyone has the right to speak with gentle speech. Everyone has a duty to listen with compassion and try to be free from preconceived ideas and prejudices.

My community is really made up of many communities. There are two temples for monks and laymen. There are two temples for nuns and laywomen. Everyone practices Beginning Anew at least once a week. We sit in a circle, and inside the circle there is a flower pot with only one flower. We start by sitting silently to practice mindful breathing and to be aware that we have a chance to sit together as a family, as a community and to feel the presence of each other. It is very important that we recognize the people who are associated with us in our life, in our duty, and in our work. We have to be a good team. We have to be a good community before we can serve the people outside.

Then the one who wants to speak will join his or her palms. That is our tradition, but you don't need to join your palms if you are not used to this. You can make up some other kind of symbol that indicates you wish to speak. Then everyone else responds with a smile and that same gesture. When we join our palms together, that is our sign that the other person should go ahead and begin. And then you mindfully and slowly stand up and do walking meditation to the center of the circle, breathing in and out mindfully, peacefully. Bow to the flower, remove it, and go back to your seat and sit down. You are holding the flower, which symbolizes that you are committed to expressing yourself and communicating to the circle. You try to remain fresh. Say everything that is in your heart, but say it while practicing loving speech. You want to retain your calm and freshness as you speak. The flower in your hands and the people around you help you to do that.

While you are holding the flower and speaking, no one else has the right to speak. No one has the right to cut in. Of course there is a code of behavior that you should not take all the time of the community. You should be considerate. Take a reasonable time to do your job, being mindful that there are other brothers or other sisters sitting there who also need to practice.

The first thing you do is to practice expressing gratitude. We call this "flower watering." You look at those around you and identify the good things in them and express gratitude and appreciation for something they have done. You water the seed of happiness in everyone. Everyone has his or her own weakness, but everyone has his or her own strengths. So the first thing is to express your happiness, your gratitude for the good things you have received, the positive things that have happened to the community during the last seven days. If you are a beginner, it may be difficult to find the good things to say. But if you are used to it, it's not so difficult. You can touch the best things in the other people, and you can transform the atmosphere with your speech.

After you've finished expressing appreciation, you can start the second part, where you express regret. You may regret that during the past week you have been unmindful, or you may have spoken harsh words. You may have been rude to a colleague. It is very good that you express your regrets, because that will encourage others to do the same. That is de-escalation of anger. If you only accuse, then anger will come up. This is very important. As human beings we are not perfect. We have shortcomings. We have times when we are not mindful. We have said things or done things that may have caused painful feelings. This is a time to practice expressing regrets. The sisters and brothers in Plum Village always find regrets to express. This will bring down the level of anger and hatred very quickly.

After this, you can begin to express hurt. You may have been hurt by the behavior of a brother, sister, or colleague during the past week. You may have tried hard to practice to transform the hurt. If you have been able to transform it, then you have realized that when you get hurt, it has more to do with the seed of anger and misunderstanding inside you than with the other person. Then you can express right away: "I'm sorry. When you said that, I was very angry and I thought that my suffering has been caused only by you. But after a few days of practice I realized that I was mainly responsible for my anger and my suffering, and you were only a minor cause. So I apologize that at that moment I blamed everything on you, which is not correct." But if by the end of the week, you have not been able to transform the hurt, then you have to be honest. You say: "I have tried my best but I have not succeeded. So please explain to me, my colleague, my friend, my sister, why you have done such a thing to me. It makes me suffer."

Then the last part is to propose something that will be to bring more harmony and happiness to the community. This is a very wonderful practice. It makes the atmosphere easy to breathe again. It brings air into the community. It reestablishes communication. If you can practice Beginning Anew every week, transformation and healing will continue to happen.

There are young people who get married in Plum Village. And we always tell them to practice Beginning Anew every week, even the first week after the wedding when they are still very happy, when they still don't have any problem with each other. Their happiness is so great that they can ignore the minor irritation. But if they ignore the minor irritation, and it continues to accumulate, then there will come a time when they cannot deal with it anymore. This is why right after the wedding they have to begin the weekly practice of Beginning Anew. If there is no problem, then they just practice flower watering in order to increase the awareness of happiness.

Suppose, during the reception, the young husband had said something that was not entirely true. He was boasting a little bit, exaggerating the truth in order to impress people. The wife did not think it was correct—what he said was true, but not completely true. He exaggerated in order to impress people. So during the time she listened to him, she lost some of her respect, because she thought her husband was not telling the whole truth, because of his need to impress people. When you lose some respect toward the person you love, there is a danger, because true love can only be maintained when there is respect. The moment you lose some respect for the person you love, your love is threatened. This is why even if the happiness is still tremendous, during the session of Beginning Anew, she has to tell him: "Dear one, during the party you said something that I don't think is completely true. Did you have the intention of impressing people? I suffer a little bit. I want you to be completely honest and correct because my love is based on my trust in you." She may be wrong in her perception. So her husband can help her by saying: "Well that's the truth. I told the truth." Then she can correct her perception. But if her husband recognizes that he has gone a little bit too far, then he says: "I exaggerated a little bit. I promise that I will not do it again." Then the internal knot in the young wife will be untied.

⊷§

In whatever field you work, you can organize Beginning Anew and persuade your colleagues to do this every week. It's very important to go back to yourself as a community and identify the suffering and the difficulties, and try to hold them with your mindfulness and compassion in order for them to heal and transform.

Every week you have to do this. Do not leave anything that jeopardizes your happiness and trust. This can be done in the community of practice. This practice is never a waste of time. If you are influential in your department, in your organization, in your administration, please persuade other members to agree to this kind of practice. Every week you have to come together to discuss the problem, not only for the well-being and happiness of your community, but for survival, because without this, you have no support. You don't have enough nourishment to go out and serve the people you want to serve.

Make your school or police department a model for the rest of the country. You could start a pilot community, practice Beginning Anew, and learn to deal with each other as real brothers and sisters existing within a community. In very little time, the atmosphere in the department will change completely. There will be mutual understanding and a real sense of community. And if you continue to practice, this will continue to grow. Your community grows from and supports the practice.

7 Getting Help

Workplace Practice: Right Thought and Right Speech

"THERE ARE SO MANY THINGS I DON'T SAY AT WORK.
MY PARTNER TELLS ME I TALK IN MY SLEEP, SAYING ALL
THE THINGS I CAN'T SAY DURING THE DAY."
—*Social Worker, Boulder, Colorado*

FREDERICK was a businessperson who believed that everything he did was for his wife and children's well-being. He really believed that, but in reality, his wife and children suffered. His wife, Claudia, felt lonely. She felt her husband did not really see her. She was not embraced by his attention. She did not feel understood by him, nor did she feel his love. She tried to hide her loneliness with friends, consumption, and charitable activities, but the feelings still surfaced. She asked Frederick to slow down, but he believed that he was doing the right thing by working so hard. He believed he was doing it for his wife, for his children, and for the people he worked with in his firm. His success gave him a sense of accomplishment, but mostly he was thinking about the future—about how he would advance in the firm and be able to enjoy his retirement.

But Frederick did not have the chance to grow old. He died after a car accident at the age of fifty-one. He never had a chance to retire. For much of his life, he was not really fully alive, because he was not living in the present moment. Not only did he himself suffer because of this, but he also caused suffering for the people he loved.

LOOKING INTO OUR THINKING

Most of our thinking in our daily lives carries us away from the present moment. We get lost in the past and the future. This kind of thinking prevents us from being truly alive. In this context we can say: "I think, therefore I am not there." But there is also positive thinking that helps us look into the nature of things and understand the present moment.

In Buddhism, we call this kind of thinking "right thinking." What is right thinking? It is the kind of thinking that helps you to understand more deeply, to be loving, to be compassionate, to be free. Right thinking reflects our deep understanding of reality. Right thinking reflects a situation as it is, free from wrong perceptions. It is possible to train ourselves to set our thinking right.

When painters creates pieces of art, they always sign their names. In your daily life you produce thinking, speech, and action. Your thoughts are your creation and they always bear your name. If your thinking is right thinking, it is a good work of art. If you can produce a thought that is in the direction of understanding and compassion, that is your creation, your legacy. Looking into your thinking, whether it is right or wrong, we see your signature. This is why in our daily life we have to be careful to produce thoughts that are in line with right thinking. You have an opportunity to produce right thinking in every moment of your life. It is what you transmit to your children and to the world.

Everything you say is also a product of your person. What you say may cause a lot of anger, despair, and pessimism, and that, too, bears your signature. With mindfulness, you can produce loving thought and speech that will bear your signature.

When you have right thinking, and when you have enough peace and happiness within you, then everything you say will carry with it these positive elements and will help water the good seeds in other people. If talking is only for the purpose of complaining, expressing your anger, frustration, and violence, then you will do harm to yourself and to others.

Mindful conversation is our practice. When we speak, we should know the effect that conversation will have on us and on other people. If we practice mindfulness of speech, then we will know whether our conversation is watering the good seeds in us, or whether we are watering the seeds of suffering. With that mindfulness, we can intervene, saying: "Dear friend, let us be aware that talking like that is watering the negative seeds in both of us. It's not healthy. Let us try to talk about things that can bring more hope and joy." This is always possible.

Suppose your relationship with your coworker is suffering. You and your coworker are angry with each other over a perceived slight, a promotion, or a time when the other person did not acknowledge you. You may blame everything on the other person. You think that it is only you who suffers, that the other person does not suffer. You believe they are responsible for your suffering. This is not right thinking. You are co-responsible for the difficulty in the relationship. A relationship is between two people who, like all of us, are connected to each other. The other person's part of the misunderstanding cannot exist without your part.

We can transform our thinking by practicing mindfulness. When you practice mindfulness, you become more aware of yourself. When anger comes up, you know anger is there. So you practice mindful breathing and you say: "Breathing in, I know anger is in me. Breathing out, I will take good care of my anger." And if you practice according to this teaching, you won't be reactive, you won't be tempted to immediately say or do anything to the person with whom you are angry. Saying or doing something in anger will only be destructive. Go home and continue to practice mindful breathing and mindful walking. Embrace your anger, recognize it, and bring relief to your anger. And after that you can look deeply into your anger and ask why you are angry.

Maybe, because we have wrong ideas, the seed of anger is too big in us. This is why as soon as we hear or see something that is not pleasant, the seed of anger in us is watered, and we become angry. We are the main cause of our suffering. The other person is just a secondary cause. If we know that, we are less angry. If we look deeply into our anger we see that it has been made by wrong perceptions, wrong views, and misunderstanding. When we realize that, our anger is transformed.

We have to make a commitment to ourselves and our work communities, that from now on every time anger manifests, we will not do anything or say anything.

If we are not capable of transforming our anger, then we have to tell the person with whom we are angry and ask for help. This should be done after we have tried being alone with our anger, but not so long that the anger has had time to solidify. Usually, it is best to communicate anger within twenty-four hours, because it's not healthy to keep anger inside if we cannot resolve it.

Let the other person know that you are angry, you suffer, and you don't know why the other person has said or done this thing. Ask for help and explanation. If you are so angry that you cannot tell him or her directly, write it down.

I want you to write down these sentences in order to practice:

The first sentence you write down is: "Dear colleague or friend: I suffer. I am angry. I want you to know it." That is the first sentence. Because your lives are connected, you have the duty to tell the other person what you are feeling.

The second sentence is: "I am doing my best." This means that I am practicing mindful breathing, I have refrained from saying things and doing things out of anger and instead I am looking deeply and trying to practice right thought and right speech. That second sentence inspires a lot of respect in the other person, and he or she will try to practice also.

The third sentence is: "Please help me." You may want to elaborate and say: "Because I cannot deal with this anger alone. I have practiced. But almost twenty-four hours have passed, and I only get a little bit of relief. I cannot transform alone. Please help me."

Asking for help is a wonderful thing. Usually, when you get hurt, you are inclined to say: "I don't need you. I don't need your help. I can survive all alone." And you get more angry. If you can bring yourself to write that sentence: "Please help me," then your anger will subside right away. Instead of trying to cope alone, do the opposite. Say, "I need you. I suffer. Please come and help."

I propose that everyone who wants to have more happiness in their work life, and in their home life, memorize these three sentences. You may like to write down these sentences on a piece of paper and slip it into your wallet. It's a bell of mindfulness. Every time anger comes up, the first thing you can do is take your wallet out and read these three sentences. These sentences are the Buddha, your teacher, and your best friend, telling you exactly what to do and exactly what not to do, and then you will be reminded of your practice.

SECTION 3

Peace in the World

8 A Safe Place

Workplace Practice: A Code of Ethics

"IF I DIDN'T CREATE ORDER IN MY CLASSROOM AND HAVE
SET STANDARDS OF BEHAVIOR, IT WOULD BE CHAOS. BUT I TRY
AND CREATE STANDARDS AND ETHICS THAT THE KIDS CAN
UNDERSTAND AND AGREE TO AS FAIR."
—*Teacher, Boulder, Colorado*

IN PLUM VILLAGE, we have several hundred monks, nuns, and laypeople practicing together as an organism. We have a code of behavior called the Mindfulness Trainings. This code is as old as the Buddha and has been passed down for thousands of years, but it is not imposed on us by anyone. It is something we have all agreed to for our own happiness.

As an individual, you may have a code of behavior to protect yourself. Similarly, your family and your workplace may have some agreed upon kinds of practice to protect yourselves as a family or a community. Maybe you all agree to sit together quietly before meals or to sit by yourselves, if you are angry, before talking with another person. These mutual agreements can protect and nourish you and your family or your work community.

To function as an organism, there must be a code of behavior that everyone is willing to accept. You cannot just use the authority of a father or a mother to oblige a child to do something. If they are doing something that is harming your family, you have to explain this to them with loving kindness. You cannot just write down a few laws like: "Don't come home after such and such an hour;" "You should spend only that much money;" or "When your father talks to you, you have to listen and not reply right away." All these things may be helpful, but they are not enough. The code of behavior has to be created and practiced in such a way that communication between everyone in the family becomes possible and joyful.

It is the same way in a work environment. Just because you supervise people at work, it does not work to create orders and force people to follow them. As a teacher, I don't use my authority to force my students to do what I want them to do. It doesn't work. Instead, I sit down with my students and show them that their negative behavior or action is not bringing happiness either to them or to the community.

Many of us are schoolteachers. The school should be a place where the practice of mindfulness can be an agent for protection and healing. Many students come from families and situations that are hard. Many teachers have also had their own difficult experiences that they bring into the classroom. Often, both students and teachers bring their own troubles to school and worsen each other's suffering. To practice mindfulness is to have a code of ethics that creates a safe place for the collective energy of mindfulness to embrace people who are suffering. It takes a lot of patience to accept them and give them a chance to transform.

For me, understanding is the very foundation of love. If you don't understand others' difficulties, suffering, pain, and deepest aspirations, you cannot truly care for them and make them happy. This is why understanding *is* love. Do you have the time to look and to understand? Do you understand yourself? Do you understand the roots of your own suffering, your own pain and sorrow? Do you know how to handle yourself with compassion? If you do not know how to handle yourself with compassion and understanding, how can you relate to others with understanding and compassion? This is the kind of practice that can promote a code of behavior that will make the work place harmonious, happy, and peaceful.

So teachers, police officers, social workers, and all of us who are frequently in contact with people who are suffering need to learn how to handle our own anger and frustration. When we are frustrated, we can say: "Breathing in, I know that anger is in me. Breathing out, I am holding my anger with tenderness. I should not make my students or clients suffer because of my anger, even if some of them behave in a very violent way."

AGREEMENT RATHER THAN AUTHORITY

When a young police officer says: "I love being a cop," it may be that he simply enjoys his job as a police officer and wants to help people. But it may also be that he enjoys the authority he has. People respect him as a police officer, and he enjoys that. But if he does not practice, later on he will suffer. The training of police officers should include training on how not to identify yourself, your ego, with the power bestowed on you as a police officer. This is very important.

If you are training police officers, teachers, or anyone in a position of authority, you should make it clear right in the beginning that authority is not there to be abused.

Especially in Buddhist countries, monks are treated with much reverence and respect, even bowed to. If we don't practice understanding that we are not our robes, that we are not the authority, we fall victim to our egos and make ourselves and our communities suffer. We have failed in our lives as monks. The robe of a monk represents the Dharma. When you become a monk, you make the vow to embody the Dharma, to make the Dharma into the ultimate aim of your life. If someone bows before you, if they show utmost respect before you, don't think that they are worshiping you, your ego. If you do, you are lost. There are times when thousands of people bow to me with utmost respect. But because of the practice of mindfulness, I know that they are bowing to the Dharma. They are bowing to the good, the true, and the beautiful. They do not bow to my ego. And I remain free. I protect myself with the energy of mindfulness. If I am caught in pride, if I have the wrong thinking, the wrong understanding, the wrong perception of their worship, I die as a monk.

Every time a young person becomes a monk or a nun and is given a robe to wear, right away I tell him or her to practice letting go of ego. If you wear the robe of a monk you will be the object of veneration and respect of many people. Don't think that they are showing their respect and veneration to you, your ego. No. You may still have a lot of anger, ignorance, and hatred in you. They are not bowing to your ego; they are bowing to the symbol of truth and beauty that you represent. But you cannot say: "No, no, no, I am not worthy of your respect." You have no right to do that, because you wear the robe. So the only thing you can do is just sit very quietly, breathing in and out, and become aware that they are bowing to truth and beauty, the Dharma, and you are safe.

❧ Workplace Practice: A Code of Ethics

When you wear a robe, you become the symbol of the Dharma, just as when you put on a police officer's uniform, you become a symbol of the law, or when you sit behind a teacher's desk you become the symbol of authority. This can be a danger, but it also gives you the opportunity to think about how to work together with people to create a code of ethics in a community.

If you are training police officers, teachers, doctors, or social workers, please tell them right away that if people show them a lot of respect and fear, they are showing it to the law, to medicine, to education. They are showing their respect to the code of behavior and not to you as an individual. If you feel you need people to show deference and you enjoy it wrongly, you will suffer later on, and the suffering may spread to your department, or to your family.

That does not mean that you cannot enjoy being a person who serves society. Power has been conferred on you so that you can be of service. You can help protect people, offer them safety, and help them heal the violence in them so that they will not lash out. That person who holds the gun, who is about to shoot, he is also the object of your service. If you can prevent him or her from shooting, you are doing him or her a good service. And you do that out of compassion. You don't consider them your enemy. If you consider them your enemy, this is not in the line of right thinking. Not only do you serve the peaceful citizens, you also serve the potential criminals. Your job is to prevent violence.

If you engage in a power struggle with those you serve, you can never unite happily as a community. If you let go of this need for authority, it is possible for police officers, schoolteachers, corrections officers to live happily as a school, a department, a community, and to enjoy the understanding and the support of the people outside.

How do you create a mutual code of ethics with those you serve? There should be time for teachers and students to sit down together and talk to each other about their difficulty, their suffering. Mutual understanding will remove anger and hatred, and teachers and students will behave like members of the same family. Transformation and healing can be obtained in school because school has become a second chance, a second family. If teachers and students succeed, they will be able to bring the healing home to their family.

This is harder to do in police professions, but it is possible. I imagine that the police department can organize open houses and invite the people in the area to come and meet them as human beings, capable of dancing, of singing, of being gentle and happy. The police department magazines should be filled with positive articles, stories, and poems, so that there is mutual understanding between the police officers and the people they want to serve. And I think we, as civilians, should occasionally organize a party and invite our police officers to come and enjoy a concert, music, or dancing, so we can see the humanity of the police officer. This is very important. This is not impossible. Once we see each other as human beings, we can realize we have shared goals, hopes, and ethics.

9 Cultivating Compassion

Workplace Practice: Looking with the Eyes of Compassion

"AS POLICE OFFICERS, WE RESPOND TO PEOPLE IN CRISIS THAT HAVE NOWHERE ELSE TO TURN. IN MANY WAYS, WE'RE SOCIAL WORKERS WITH GUNS. AND IT'S VERY HARD FOR US, BECAUSE SOMETIMES WE HAVE TO MAKE SPLIT SECOND DECISIONS. AND THEN PEOPLE GET MONTHS TO THINK ABOUT WHETHER OR NOT WE MADE THE RIGHT DECISION. AND SO WE END UP FEELING VERY DEFENSIVE."
—*Police Sergeant, Madison, Wisconsin*

I HAVE A FRIEND who is a police officer in Los Angeles. One day, he was called to the home of a lady who was mentally ill. When he opened the door he saw the lady shouting and holding a knife, and he shot her. She was only holding a knife. And she was mentally sick. If the police officer had had enough understanding, compassion, and peace he wouldn't have had to use his gun. But because he had not practiced, he had allowed violence, fear, and hatred to invade him. Now, he practices mindfulness regularly, but it took this situation to make him realize what was going on inside him.

With enough serenity and peace, we can avoid a lot of violent situations. Wearing a smile, we can say: "Hello! How are you? Can I help you? Is anything wrong? I am here to help you." With our warmth and our compassion, we may be able to transform a person or move a situation towards a peaceful resolution.

Of course, you have to make use of every means to protect yourself. But you have to look deeply in order to see that outside the means of protection you are aware of, you may have other means of protection that are more important. During the Buddha's lifetime, he came across a feared and violent killer, Angulimala. Angulimala had killed many people and when he saw the Buddha, he screamed at him to stop. The Buddha explained that he had already stopped; he had stopped hating and killing and now it was time for Angulimala to do the same. The Buddha did not have a gun to deal with Angulimala, but he was not fearful at all. He trusted his ability to act with intelligence, compassion, and skillfulness and his words disarmed the killer.

Police officers, teachers, social workers, and other people who deal with violence should arm themselves with compassion, intelligence, and lucidity. These are the best means to protect yourself. I do not mean to suggest that police officers should not carry guns, but we must create an environment where they do not rely so heavily on them. You have to rely on your intelligence, your compassion, your understanding. If you have these elements in you, everyone can become your friend, including the potential criminals. Don't look at these potential criminals as the enemy; look at them as the objects of your help and service. If you can stop a person before he or she executes the crime, you are helping. Without you, this person might kill or destroy and have to serve time in prison.

CHOOSING A BETTER WEAPON

It is time to look with the eyes of compassion. Your job is to protect everyone, the potential criminals as well as the potential victims of their crimes. We suffer only because we don't know how to look with the eyes of compassion.

You may be concerned that if you are compassionate you won't be safe. You may feel you have to choose between protecting yourself and being compassionate, but the opposite is true. When you have compassion and serenity in you, you can see the situation much more clearly. When you are aware of what is going on, without judging it, you are able to see clearly.

Compassion and mindfulness allow us to be aware of what is really going on. Suppose you have pulled over a car. It may be that everyone in the car seems normal and happy. You can see their hands and see that no one is hiding a gun. This kind of awareness helps you to smile and to say something pleasant to the people in the car, even as you are doing your job.

When you do this, the people in the car can recognize you as a human being, with the capacity of feeling sadness and joy. Even if you need to take the person out of the car and search the person or the car, it can be done with mindfulness and compassion. It helps if you are not alone. If you have a colleague standing vigilantly and mindfully behind you, you can do these things in a very friendly way. It is possible. You don't have to be rude. You don't have to be afraid. You can do it with all your lucidity, your stability, and your gentleness.

We have many better weapons than the gun. We have our mindfulness, we have our vigilance, we have our compassion, and we have our skillfulness. In one moment, you can transform a situation and make it easier for both sides—the public servant and the person who is about to commit an act of violence.

It is also possible for corrections officers and other public servants to practice law enforcement in such a way as to bring relief to themselves and the people they serve. Many inmates have not had much chance to be loving and understanding. They have created a lot of suffering for other people, but it is because they have not had any happiness themselves. Nobody has helped them to be understanding and loving. They have been victims of wrong perceptions. They thought that the only way to be happy was to run after fame, power, profit, and sex. And, in desperation for these things, they committed crimes.

With understanding and compassion, we can see that these kinds of cravings make a person suffer deeply. More than any weapon, our compassion and understanding protect us from anger, fear, and despair. When we cultivate these qualities, we as public servants can suffer less. And when we are able to look at others with the eyes of compassion, they will feel it, and they too will suffer less. If they are helped, they will live their life with much less suffering and they will begin to experience some joy, even in prison.

To help cultivate compassion, it is helpful to visualize the other person's life. Here is an example from my own life. In the late seventies in Vietnam, many people could not accept the policies of the new government, so they fled on boats. The boat people were trying to reach another country, but because of the storms, many of them died on the ocean. Many of them fell victim to sea pirates who robbed them of what they had and raped the women and girls. Many of the sea pirates came from Thailand, and they were largely poor fishermen.

One day in my hermitage in France, I received a letter from the director of a refugee camp in Thailand telling me that an eleven-year-old girl had been raped by a pirate on her refugee boat. Her father had tried to intervene, but the sea pirate threw him into the ocean and he died. After she was raped, the girl also jumped into the ocean and died with her father. When I received this letter I had to go into the nearby woods and practice walking meditation to calm myself and to find ways to help victims of this kind of attack. At first, I was angry. I was angry at the pirate who had raped the young girl and thrown her father into the ocean.

That night I practiced sitting meditation and, after some time, I obtained peace. I had transformed my anger through visualization. First, I imagined myself as a little boy born in the coastal area of Thailand in the very poor family of a fisherman. My mother, the fisherman's wife, had no education. She didn't know how to raise me and never sent me to school. So I grew up as a delinquent. When I attained the age of fourteen, I had to go out and fish with my father to earn a living. My friends were like me—we had no education, and no one to help us cultivate understanding and love.

I imagined that one day, as the young fisherman, I learned that a boat full of people was passing by, and that they may possess some valuables, perhaps a gold necklace, or maybe some money. I thought that if I robbed them just one time I might get enough gold or enough money to change my life, to get out of poverty and begin the kind of life that my ancestors never had. I was tempted. When I went out on the ocean, I saw my fellow fishermen robbing and raping. I said: "There are no police here. Why don't I try once?" So I committed the crimes of raping and killing. If someone on the boat had had a gun, that person could have shot and killed me. This would have merely been punishment.

This visualization was very powerful. I know very well that if I was a police officer on that boat with a gun, I might have had to kill the young fisherman. But no one had ever helped him to be a human being, capable of understanding and love. Where were all the educators and political leaders? They had left these Thai fisherman's children without any education. They had never given them half a chance to grow up as educated people.

That night, during meditation, I visualized hundreds of babies being born along the coast of Thailand, into the families of poor fishermen. If, over the next twenty years, no one helped them, then many would become sea pirates. If I had been born into such a family twenty years before, maybe now I would be a pirate. I might lose my life because I never had a chance to learn to be a good human being. The moment I saw that, all anger in me disappeared, and I only had compassion for the young Thai pirate.

If you look at the bad student, the violent person, the rapist, you will see that most likely no one has helped them—no teacher, no parent, no public servant ever helped them. And society is organized in such a way that we produce many rapists and criminals every day. With this kind of understanding, maybe you can be freed from anger towards these criminals, and not want to punish anymore. You want to do something to help, because these criminals are also victims. You want to do something to prevent the formation of future rapists and criminals. And if you have in yourself that kind of understanding, compassion, and the great vow to do something to prevent this from happening in the future, you begin to heal and you don't have to suffer anymore.

It is possible for corrections officers to establish a friendly relationship with the prison inmates. If corrections officers become a community, if there is enough understanding and compassion in the heart of the officers, then everyone will suffer less. We will have more tools and more joy in order to handle the situation. And that will bring relief and ease to the inmates. There are many ways to communicate with them. It is possible for us as public servants to use the language of loving-kindness and to practice deep listening. We can always breathe in, breathe out, and smile. And we don't just wear a diplomatic smile, we do it authentically.

As corrections officers, we also must be of service to the families of the inmates when they come to visit the prison. We try to help them. We try to be very kind to them. And we should be able to ask for their help to handle the inmates. This is possible. With the collaboration and understanding of the prison population and their families, we will make life in prison much more comfortable and pleasant. We can even help shorten the terms many inmates have to serve. You may think the inmates don't deserve these things, because they have hurt others. But with the eyes of compassion, you see that there is no need to add to suffering. The practice of mindfulness brings about deep understanding, mutual understanding, and compassion that could transform the prison into a place where there is love and understanding.

10 Feeding the Hungry Ghosts

Workplace Practice: Deep Listening and Loving Speech

"IF JUST ONE PERSON SMILES AT ME AND THANKS ME,
IT CHANGES MY WHOLE DAY. I AM MORE ABLE TO LISTEN
AND SEE OTHER PEOPLE AND I FIND MYSELF SMILING
ON THE JOB, SOMETHING I ALMOST NEVER DO."
—*Police Officer, Madison, Wisconsin*

IN PLUM VILLAGE, we have retreats where Israelis and Palestinians can practice being together in peace. At first, they don't even look at or speak to each other. There are Israelis who believe that the Palestinians only want to kill them, that they don't want their existence as a people and as a nation. And there are Palestinians who believe that the Israelis only want to kill them, and don't want to let their existence as a people or a nation. When people have wrong perceptions like this, their actions are influenced by hatred and fear. When you suffer, you want to punish. When you are being punished, you want to retaliate. This causes an escalation of violence, anger, and suspicion.

When Israelis and Palestinians come to Plum Village, the first thing we offer them is the practice of mindful walking and breathing, to recognize their pain, suffering, and suspicion. Then, when they are able to smile, we ask them to sit down and listen to each other with our support.

Only the practices of deep listening and loving speech can help both sides to understand each other's suffering and remove wrong perceptions.

People who commit violent acts have wrong views of themselves and they have wrong views about the people they attack. The people who flew the planes into the World Trade Center and the Pentagon believed that the United States did not like them, their country, or their religion. They may have thought of the United States as anti-Islamic or anti-Arab. Believing that the United States was trying to destroy them, they were ready to die in order to punish the U.S.

We know that the basis of terrorism and violence is wrong perception. Are we capable of talking to the people with whom we are at war and removing their wrong perceptions? We know we cannot remove wrong perceptions by using guns or bombs. As citizens of the United States, we must find loving speech in order to resolve misperceptions. We must acknowledge that we have been viewed as evil, as having the intention to destroy a nation, a religion and a culture. We must ask how we, as individuals, can change the perception that the United States wishes to destroy Arab or Islamic people. And we must listen to their response.

This is loving speech, inviting the people to express themselves. We must be honest, we must be open, and we must be ready to listen. And when you listen deeply with compassion, you understand what kind of wrong perceptions they have about themselves and about us. And by listening deeply we may recognize that we, too, have had wrong perceptions about ourselves and about them. Communication helps both sides to remove wrong impressions.

Some people may respond with cynicism and suspicion because they have met with negative situations in the past. They don't trust others easily. They have not received enough understanding and love. They suspect that what we offer them is not authentic love, authentic compassion. Even if we really do have love and understanding to offer, they still suspect us. There are many young people who have not gotten understanding and love from their family, their parents, their teachers, society. They don't see anything beautiful, true, and good. So they are wandering around, seeking something to believe in. They wander around like hungry ghosts.

From time to time we see hungry ghosts coming to our community. The way they walk, the way they look, we feel that they are really ghosts. We do have enough compassion and understanding to offer them, but it's not easy for them to accept. We have to be very patient. They are like trees without roots. It's not easy for them to take in the nutrients that they need. Patience is part of compassion. If you are really compassionate, you have the capacity to wait.

In the Buddhist tradition, we describe a hungry ghost as having a big belly—very hungry, and a very tiny throat, like a needle. They are very hungry, but while their belly has plenty of room, their capacity for swallowing food is very tiny. Hungry ghosts are like that. They are hungry for love and understanding, and yet their capacity to receive love and understanding is very little. You have to help bring the size of their throat back to normal before they can swallow the food that you offer. That is the practice of patience, continued lovingkindness, and understanding. It takes time to win their trust. Until then you cannot help them. That is why even if you are faced with cynicism or suspicion, you have to continue with your practice.

Creating a Safe Environment

If you have a community, you can set up an environment where two sides that have seen each other as enemies can come to find calm and practice embracing their pain and their sorrow, so that they can sit down and listen to each other. There is no hurry to arrive at a peaceful resolution. The most important thing is the practice of calming down, so that people have enough lucidity to listen and to understand.

When we have learned that the other side suffers just like us, that they and their children are victims of suspicion, anger, fear, and death, then we begin to understand that we are all victims of the conflict. And we all want to live in peace. To continue to punish each other is a mad course of action. When we begin to understand, then our own wrong perceptions are removed. Now you can look at the other group with sympathy.

When the Israelis and Palestinians have listened to each other and communicated in Plum Village, they return to the Middle East and establish communities of practice, and invite other people to join. We are able to make change on a small scale. But it has proven to be effective. If our governments apply the techniques, creating an atmosphere of peace, helping people to calm down, helping them to sit down and listen to each other, that is a much better way to remove terrorism and war than the way of war and force.

In 2004, the United States spent about four billion dollars a month in Iraq. Organizing a retreat costs much less. And there are those like us who are ready to come and help organize a nonsectarian retreat that would provide a safe and open place in which citizens of the warring nations can engage in dialogue.

Sometimes, tensions in the workplace or tension between the people you work with and the people you serve, can become so strong that it feels as if you are entering a war just by going to work. But if Palestinians and Israelis can talk together, surely people at work can too. We know that every one of us can be an inspiration for reconciliation and peace. Every one of us can be a bodhisattva, a Buddha.

Every one of us, whether we are psychotherapists, judges, lawyers, teachers, police officers, corrections officers, parents, daughters, or sons can work a little bit in order to apply these practices of deep listening and loving speech. These two techniques are the only instruments that can restore communication. When communication is there, everything is possible. Communication helps remove wrong perceptions. Wrong perceptions are the base of all hatred, fear, violence, and terrorism.

Deep listening is a wonderful practice. It simply means listening with compassion. Even if the other person is full of wrong perceptions, discrimination, blaming, judging, you are still capable of sitting quietly and listening. Because you know that if you can listen like that for one hour, the other person will get relief. You remember that to listen like this has only one purpose: to give the other person a chance, because so far no one has taken the time to listen. Now you are a bodhisattva of listening. This is a practice of compassion. And if you can keep compassion alive in you, you will not become irritated. Compassion protects you from getting irritated or angry when you hear things that are unjust, full of blaming, bitterness, and so on. It's wonderful. You can keep compassion alive in you with this kind of awareness: by listening like this, you give someone a chance. It's so simple. You keep breathing in and out, and maintain awareness, and you can listen for a long time without the seed of anger in you being touched.

If at some point you feel that the anger or irritation is beginning to arise, then you know that your capacity for compassionate listening is not strong enough. You can still practice loving speech. You can bow and say: "I think I am not in very good form today. Would you allow me another chance, maybe the day after tomorrow? I will continue to listen to you." Don't make too much effort. If your quality of listening is not good, then he or she will feel it, so don't try too hard. There are those who after only four days of practice are capable of doing compassionate listening and reestablishing dialogue and communication with their partner, friend, or colleague. I have seen a multitude of cases like that in our retreats.

When you speak, you have the right to share everything in your heart, provided that you use loving speech. When you speak lovingly, the block of pain or anger in you may come up, and it may be heard in your voice. In that case you know that your capacity for loving speech is not good enough and you say: "Would you give me another chance? Today I am not my best." And you take a few more days to practice mindful breathing, mindful walking, so that you can learn to practice loving speech.

11 Bringing the Practice to Others

Workplace Practice: Being a Bodhisattva

"[I'VE LEARNED TO] AT LEAST ATTEMPT COMPASSION
WITH EVERYONE THAT I DEAL WITH. AND IF COMPASSION
DOESN'T WORK TO CALM A PERSON DOWN, THEN [I HAVE TO]
HAVE COMPASSION FOR MYSELF AND NOT BLAME MYSELF
WHEN PEOPLE MAKE THE CHOICE TO STILL HAVE ANGER
TOWARDS ME. [I HAVE TO] TREAT MYSELF WELL WHEN I GET
HOME SO THAT I CAN STILL BE A GOOD PERSON ON THE JOB."
—*Peace Officer, Madison, Wisconsin*

THERE WAS A NUN who was a disciple of mine who had gradu-
ated from the University of Indiana with a major in English literature. She was put in prison because she had circulated literature on
peace and human rights. She spent time with the inmates and taught
them how to enjoy sitting and walking. She became like a bodhisattva. She did not suffer in prison. She brought joy and relief to other
prisoners. There are those of us who would like to do the same. We
want to go there and live with them, help them to suffer less, and give
them a chance to transform and heal. Prisons are places to practice
love and understanding. They are a place where everyone, guards and
inmates, visitors, and police officers, can be transformed.

HOW TO LESSEN SUFFERING

As a corrections officer, why don't you use your time on the job to practice looking deeply? Is there anything you can do to help others to suffer less? Is it possible for inmates in the prison to practice so that they can suffer less? Can they help each other in the practice of bringing hope and joy to their life in prison? Of course the answer is yes.

I have visited prisons and spent time with prisoners. Many prisoners told me directly that in prison they can practice joy, they can practice transformation and healing, they can help other inmates, and their life begins to have meaning. As a corrections officer, you can help make that happen. You can offer yourself as an agent of transformation and healing for the inmates. You can offer your service to transform the situation of your colleagues and to build friendship and brotherhood. There are many things we can do. Why don't you enjoy fifteen minutes of walking meditation? Maybe you can begin your shift with fifteen minutes of walking meditation, touching the Earth with your feet, touching the fresh air, the stars, aware that the wonders of life are there for you and others. If you know the joy of walking meditation, then spend some time just enjoying walking to nourish your body and your mind. And later on you might talk to the inmates and share your practice, expressing your loving kindness and your intention to help them suffer less. Build human relationships; this is something that all of us can do.

The nun who went to prison and helped the people in the prison practice mindful walking, mindful sitting, embracing their anger, is called a bodhisattva. As a corrections officer you can become a bodhisattva, easing the suffering of the inmates and your colleagues. All of them become the object of your service. Your life has a meaning. You may like to spend fifteen minutes in sitting meditation. You are fully there, fully present for them in your walking, in your sitting. And you do it for love. You do it not only for yourself, but for them also. Your presence here is very important. Simply by practicing right thinking, you change your situation.

There's always something you can do. You might read a book. You might listen to a talk that can water the seeds of joy, understanding, and compassion in you. You may like to learn more about art, about the mysteries of life, about civilization. There is a thirst for learning, for understanding, for loving, in every one of us. The deepest desire in every human being is to know more, to learn more, and to be able to love. During your seven hours of duty you can cultivate the need to understand and to love, and allow it to be satisfied. The seven hours can be very fulfilling, very beautiful, if only you know how to do it. And during your shift, you can cultivate your joy, your compassion, and your understanding. Then you can offer that joy, understanding, and compassion for the transformation of the inmates and the corrections community.

If you learn this as a teacher or a corrections officer, you can share it with students or inmates. A corrections officer can talk in a friendly way to the inmates in prison, and give them instructions on how to enjoy mindful breathing and mindful walking. You can share your own experience with mindfulness as an example. A police officer, a social worker, and a teacher can do this in the same way.

You, as a public servant, can be a bodhisattva, and your life will be filled with joy and hope. If you know how to bring understanding and compassion into yourself, you will help transform our society. First of all you have transformed yourself, and you have transformed your department, your community, your administration. Together you can bring relief and transformation into the life of the inmates.

As a police officer you can be a bodhisattva, an enlightened being filled with understanding and compassion, capable of being joyful, and smiling, because you have peace within yourself. A police officer is someone who is supposed to bring peace—a peace officer—because your duty is to maintain peace. Peace means the absence of conflict, violence, and anger. You should have peace within yourself in order to truly be doing the work of peace. Making peace is not possible without being peace. And being peace is your practice, recognizing the violence, the fear, and the anger in you, embracing them and transforming them. Get in touch with the wonderful, healing, and nourishing things around and inside you, and nourish your family and community. That should be your daily practice. As an officer, you can be seen as a human being, capable of loving, understanding, and protecting.

This is the image of police officers we must create. We need to see each other as human beings, capable of being peaceful, lucid, and compassionate. If you are a public servant, we trust you. If you act only on the basis of your fear and your anger, we will not trust you. That is why the practice of peace is so important in the community of police officers, corrections officers, psychotherapists, doctors, teachers, and others who hold the public trust.

◈ Workplace Practice: Being a Bodhisattva

If an officer has made a mistake, the community of officers should be able to embrace him, console him, and help him. They should not give him the feeling of being isolated and guilty. Because what happens to one of us happens to all of us. We are an organism; we are a community. We don't use our power to punish and blame each other. Without building a community in which harmony and brotherhood exist, we have no chance to succeed in our careers. We monks and nuns live a very simple life, without cars, bank accounts, or luxuries. We do not suffer because of that kind of simple living. In fact we are very happy, because we know that we have each other. We are sustained by the practice of cultivating brotherhood and sisterhood. I always tell my brothers and sisters: "If there is no harmony or happiness in the community and you go out and offer a retreat, you are selling false products."

You can only help and serve the cause of transformation and healing if you have practiced transformation and healing within yourself. You can only serve the cause of peace when you have some peace within yourself. It is as simple as that. That is why in our community we have to build peace, we have to build brotherhood and mutual understanding that will sustain us and help us to go far on our path of service. The city, the state, and the government should be informed about this kind of practice and help us, support us in this practice.

If corrections officers felt a sense of community in the workplace, they would have many ideas about how to help the inmates to suffer less. The inmates inflict suffering on each other. They have a lot of anger and frustration in them. When you have succeeded in your practice as a community, you can bring that practice into the population in detention and help them to do the same—the practice of Beginning Anew, loving speech, and so on. Since you practice mindful consumption and protect yourself from ingesting toxins and poisons, you can help the inmates in prison to do the same. The kind of films you allow them to see would not be the kind of films that water the seeds of violence and craving, which are already very strong in them. This is not good food for them. You try to keep them peaceful by occupying them with television and films. But by offering these kinds of films, you water the negative seeds in them, which is dangerous.

It is possible for us to select beautiful films of a highly educational nature that can help people to water the seeds of beauty, truth, and goodness. Maybe some of the officers can sit with them, explain and introduce the film to them, enjoy the film with them, and after that begin a discussion on the good things in the film. All these things will help with transformation and healing in the prison. Prison can be a place for walking meditation or tea meditation, building community and understanding, and allowing each person to express his or her own hopes and despair so that other people will understand.

I know that in some prisons, prisoners are allowed to work and earn a salary. I don't know how much they get for one hour, perhaps fifty cents. This is one method of correcting behavior. But I think making the prison into a real place of transformation and healing should be the policy of the congress and the government. We call it a correctional house. Our purpose is not to punish, but to help with transformation, to correct what is wrong. There must be an intelligent policy that can use effective means to help people to really profit from their time in prison to transform themselves and make themselves into good citizens again.

In my tradition, we believe that everyone has Buddha nature, the capacity to become a Buddha, someone with deep understanding and compassion. The killer that Buddha met in the woods also has Buddha nature. No one had helped the seed of Buddha nature in him to manifest until the moment he met the Buddha in the woods. As a corrections officer, you may be inspired to act like a Buddha. First you work for your own transformation and healing, cultivating your compassion and understanding. Then you become a bodhisattva, a Buddha, bringing the practice into your administration, your community. And then when you have succeeded in building a beautiful community, you are in a position to help the people that you serve, always bringing them the same kind of practice.

In Plum Village, we always stick together as a family and as a community. We open our center to give many retreats. This summer people came from all over the world, representing forty-seven countries. We offer retreats of mindfulness in many countries in Europe, Asia, and elsewhere. We are able to offer the practice because we have enough transformation and healing in us, enough brotherhood and joy to sustain us. Usually in retreat you need only one teacher: yourself. This is less expensive, because you only need to pay for one air ticket. But what can I do if I am alone? This is why I buy tickets for nearly one hundred monks, laypeople, and Dharma teachers to retreat together. In order to have enough of the energy of mindfulness and concentration, we need people who are already skilled in the practice, who are solid in the practice, in order to help with people who are beginners in the practice.

As an individual, you will find it difficult to convince your department or administration to follow the path. But if you are supported by a Sangha, or community of practice, you will succeed. And you may be inspired to transform your organization, your agency, or your department, into a pilot community. When you can demonstrate that the practice is successful and that you are serving people in a much

≈§

better way, other communities will learn a lot from you. This is my hope. I am optimistic. Everyone can be a Buddha, everyone can be a bodhisattva, if you are inspired by the desire to serve. You can do it, and you can begin today. Every breath, every smile, every step made in mindfulness is an act of peace, decreasing suffering and violence. It will help transform the situation and bring transformation and healing to the people who live around us, so that as a community we can go into society and help bring down the level of violence.

Please go deeply into this and share with others how to bring the practice into our community, so that our community will be the vessel for bringing peace and healing into the world.

12 Reducing Violence

"I THINK OF MY WORK AS NOT JUST REDUCING VIOLENCE,
BUT AS CREATING MORE PEACE."
—*Social Worker, Oakland, California*

HOW CAN the police officer, the school teacher, the corrections officer, the social worker, and the public official have an opportunity to participate in the work of reducing the level of violence in society? There must be ways to do so. With the practice of mindfulness in the family, in the school, in the society, in the department, in the workplace, it is possible to bring down the level of violence in us. And when we have enough mutual understanding and compassion, we will be able to help other people bring down the level of violence within themselves.

This is a time when we have to work together. If you are a journalist, you know that you can contribute positively to reducing violence. In every one of us there is a seed of fear, hatred, and despair. If you write your article or make your TV report in such a way that always waters the seeds of hate, violence, and fear in people, you are not doing your nation a service. In every one of us there are seeds of understanding, compassion, and forgiveness. If, by writing an article or making a report, you can water the seeds of patience, understanding, and compassion, you are serving your people well. Your congressmen and your government may be influenced by your way of looking. If you have lucidity and calm, you can look deeply into the situation and understand well. You will help people to better understand the situation and not allow the nation to be ruled and carried away by feelings of hate and fear. Collective hatred and fear are very dangerous; they lead to war.

LOOKING DEEPLY

Our ministries of education, our educators, and lawmakers must practice looking deeply into the nature of suffering. In order to reduce violence in the family and in school, they must create guidelines and laws that can bring about transformation and healing, rather than just suppressing violence. Violence cannot be suppressed. It will come up in many other ways.

Suppose a young person is the victim of drugs. That person is intelligent enough to know that using drugs is not good for his health and his future. But he has no alternative. Nobody helps him to handle the suffering inside. His teacher cannot, his father cannot. Left all alone, he doesn't know how to handle the suffering inside, so he has to use drugs. If you understand that, you will not punish him, even if you have to put him in jail. You have to do everything you can in order to help him transform.

Violence is overwhelming our society. The duty of corrections officers, police officers, and others is not to suppress violence, but to help truly reduce the amount of violence in society. Through the practice of transformation, officers can help reduce violence in the schools, in families, and in society. We cannot do this if we don't know how to handle the violence within ourselves. Violence is a manifestation of fear, depression, loneliness.

Addressing the Roots of Violence

In law enforcement, detention centers, and prisons, we try to suppress symptoms of violence. At the same time, we allow violence to be fed in our daily life—in our family, in our school, in our society. It does not mean much to try to suppress the symptoms. You have to deal with the roots. Suppressing violence with violence does not make any sense, because the person in charge of suppressing violence may have a lot of hatred, fear, and despair within himself.

That is why we have to reconsider our approach. We have to bring a spiritual dimension to our way of working, and of solving problems. This does not mean that we have to be religious. We have our human nature. We have our animal nature. We have our Buddha nature, our spiritual nature. It's possible that the human nature and the Buddha nature can live together with the animal nature in peace. This is called civilization. We still keep our animal nature, but it is under control. It doesn't have to suffer. We enjoy transformation and healing. We have to organize our life—individual, family, institutional, societal—in the light of that kind of insight.

We don't like terrorism. We don't like people terrorizing us, attacking us, killing us. We declare war on terrorism. We want to strike at terrorism. We want to use violence to deal with violence, to suppress symptoms of violence. Every spiritual tradition can tell you that using violence to suppress violence is not the right thing to do, because it will never bring peace. The desire to remove violence and terrorism is a good desire. It is authentic, legitimate. But the means that we use in order to remove violence and terrorism should be effective. By using violence to suppress violence we create more violence. As psychotherapists, teachers, corrections officers, police officers, if we have some time to look, we will realize that only understanding and compassion can neutralize violence. Violence only adds to violence and creates more hatred, more enemies, more terrorists. This is a fact. If you look deeply into the situation, this is clear.

We are so busy with our daily lives. We have allowed the situation to become what it is now. The situation is a collective creation of our mind. We have voted for our Congress. We have voted for our government. But we have not had the time to help them, to support them, to offer them insight. We leave everything to them. Each of us should organize our life in such a way that we have the time to be in the here and the now, to touch reality deeply, to get understanding and insight. Insight is nourishment for our life. But it is also a contribution to our society. The collective insight that we offer will serve as the light to lead the nation and the world out of this difficult situation.

TAKING COMPASSIONATE ACTION

The practices in this book can help us to bring relief to our anger and our violence. We can do the practice. But if we allow our body and our consciousness to continue to ingest more violence, our practice can only ease the symptom for a few moments. That is why we need to think globally, to have a kind of intelligence and planning to really work on the problem at the roots.

If we know that every day we can do something to reduce the level of violence in society, that knowledge can bring us a lot of comfort and healing. We know that the level of violence in society is overwhelmingly high. But if we know that in our daily life we can contribute to the work of bringing down that violence, we will feel less overwhelmed. That kind of faith, that kind of belief, that kind of understanding, will heal us. We are no longer paralyzed by the magnitude of the situation.

It is possible to do something every day to reduce the violence in society, even today. We have to sit down and find ways to do it right away. When you make a peaceful step, calming your emotions, you are already making a difference.

Every time you breathe in and out mindfully and hold your anger peacefully so that it doesn't explode into angry words, angry thinking, and angry action, that is an act of compassion that can help bring the level of violence down. Every time you can say something to calm the person in front of you, to make her smile, to help him to see things more clearly, that is an act that can help bring down the level of violence. All of us can do this today. And it brings us a feeling of relief right away that is healing and nourishing. Every one of us can begin right now. Your inner transformation will help bring peace to your family, your work environment, and your world.